Jo Frost is one of the UK's leading childcare and baby experts. Her expertise in childcare has taken her name worldwide – her television series *Supernanny* is shown in 48 countries and her books have been translated into 15 languages. Jo resides in the UK but is currently dividing her time between London and the States, where her show has become a huge success.

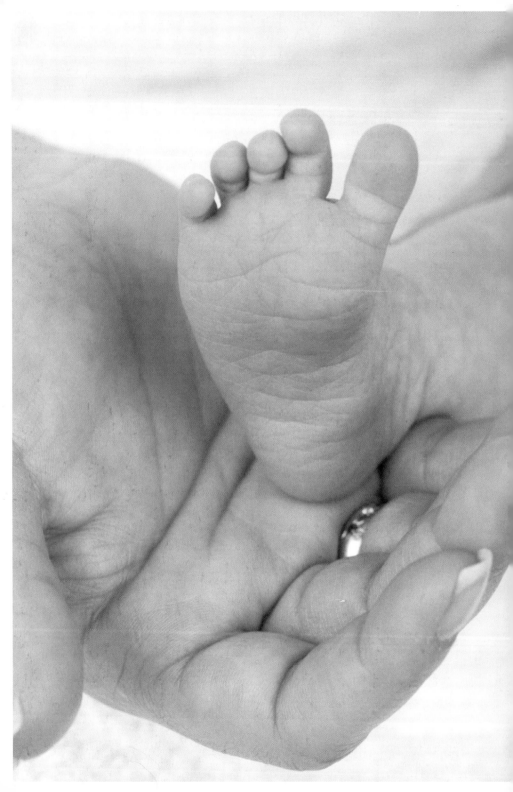

JO
FROST'S
CONFIDENT
BABY CARE

What You Need to Know for the First Year
from the UK's Most Trusted Nanny

Copyright © Jo Frost 2010

The right of Jo Frost to be identified as the author of this work
has been asserted by her in accordance with the
Copyright, Designs and Patents Act 1988.

First published in Great Britain in 2010 by
Orion Books
an imprint of the Orion Publishing Group Ltd
Orion House, 5 Upper St Martin's Lane,
London WC2H 9EA
An Hachette UK Company

1 3 5 7 9 10 8 6 4 2

A CIP catalogue record for this book is available
from the British Library.

ISBN-13: 978 1 409 10157 4

Printed and bound in Great Britain by
Butler Tanner & Dennis, Frome, Somerset

The Orion Publishing Group's policy is to use papers that are natural, renewable and recyclable
and made from wood grown in sustainable forests. The logging and manufacturing processes are
expected to conform to the environmental regulations of the country of origin.

Every effort has been made to fulfil requirements with regard to reproducing copyright material.
The author and publisher will be glad to rectify any omissions at the earliest opportunity.

www.orionbooks.co.uk

This book is dedicated to you,
so that you have what you need right
from the beginning to help your baby
grow into a loving adult.

ACKNOWLEDGEMENTS

A big thank you to:

Mary Jane, for giving me clear direction
when there was always so much to say.

Love always to those closest to my heart, who continue to support me,
the work I do and the truth behind it.

Daniel Pangbourne, the photographer, for creating the karma for such
wonderful images. Also thanks to Kevin Frazier for his contribution.

All the babies in the book: Jharrel (father and baby), Katie (bottle-feed),
Sherrall (sleeping), Chanel (gurgling), Olivia (eating), Joe (playing),
Riley (bath), twins: Teah and Sky, Keira and Kylie (reading),
Laura (hand and foot and newborn), Louis (cover). Not forgetting
Bijou, the pregnant model, and Greg in the father and baby shot.

Hair and make-up stylist Tim Alan.

Dr Mark Furman at Great Ormond St Hospital, London –
thanks for the thumbs up on the medical side of things.

Orion Publishing, for your belief in delivering this book.

Matthew Frost

Contents

Introduction

Congratulations! You're embarking on the adventure of a lifetime – having a baby. The decision to raise a fine well-adjusted child is the most serious commitment you will ever make. You're about to bring forth (or perhaps you have just brought forth) new life or, in some cases, new lives, and will be nurturing a tiny being as she grows. But what makes this so exciting is that this isn't just the birth of your child, it is the birth of your family in a new configuration. And if this is your first, it's also the birth of you as a parent. Wow!

Recently I was with friends when they brought their newborn home from hospital, and I was reminded that all the planning in the world can't prepare you for the emotion and energy that your newborn will create. You cannot imagine the feeling of holding your baby in your arms until it happens. You'll be experiencing this fabulous feeling for yourself very soon if you haven't already.

Naturally, however, you need to be prepared if you're to be the best parent you can be, so it's important to get savvy, to read up about what to expect and how to make things go as smoothly as possible. That's why I've written this book – to give the information you need to be the excellent parent you want to be. Keep it by your bedside so you can reach for it any time you need as you go through your baby's first year and it will help with any questions or concerns you might have. Think of it as your very own live-in me.

I've also written it for another important reason. No matter how many children you have, remember that this newborn, like all newborns, is a miracle. That's where the term 'bundle of joy' comes from. But as I've listened to people talking about babies over the years, I've noticed a lot of negativity – things like 'Congratulations, you're not going to sleep for years' and lots of advice about how to *cope*. My approach to baby care isn't about *coping* or dealing with strain; it's about helping you have the confidence to raise your baby in a healthy and contented way. It's also about learning just who your baby is, for each has his own soul, his own spirit, which will unfold and develop before your very eyes.

Over the last 17 years I've been with lots of families as they have brought their newborns home, and I know what a joyful one-of-a-kind experience the first year can be when you've got the right attitude, understanding and equipment. Professors, psychologists and paediatricians tell me that what they've studied for 40 years I've grasped 'in the field'. That's what I'll be sharing with you – my secrets for making your baby's first year the wonder-filled celebration it was meant to be.

That's not to say you won't experience the rough as well as the smooth. There are going to be times when you feel exhausted or cranky, overwhelmed or worried, if I didn't say that, I wouldn't be honest with you but that's all part of becoming a proud parent. Weathering the trials and tribulations along the way is how you learn. This book will help you iron out the bumpy bits so that those moments are in the minority. Your baby, your intuition and my help will be your guide.

Babies grow quickly and their needs change dramatically over the first year, which is why, after the initial section on getting prepared, I've broken Part 2 up into three-month chapters, each of which looks at:

- **Development**: the physical, mental, emotional and social growth your baby will be going through.
- **Babyproofing**: what you need to do to assure your little one's safety.
- **Setting firm ground**: routines, sleeping through the night, dealing with crying.
- **Feeding**: all the know-how, including establishing a feeding routine.
- **Parentcraft**: dressing, bathing, nappies, winding.
- **Stimulation and explorations**: activities to help with mental, physical and emotional development.

I've also included a section for parents of babies in exceptional circumstances – multiple births, premature birth and other special needs, and adopted babies – in which I discuss how you might modify my advice to your circumstances.

It's important to bear in mind that while Part 2 is divided into 0–3 months, 3–6 months, 6–9 months and 9–12 months, a baby is a living, breathing human being who grows and develops at their own pace. There aren't set cut-off points between one phase and the next. What that means, for instance, is that as your baby turns three months old, you might want to read up on the 3–6 month chapter, knowing that she's heading there fast.

I'm a realist. Instead of saying categorical things like, 'Don't heat baby's bottle in the microwave' or, 'Don't use talcum powder,' you'll be hearing whys and wherefores so that you can make the wisest choices for you. But when I feel it's absolutely crucial to do something my way, you'll hear that too.

Since the journey is as much about you as about your baby, each chapter also includes a section on your journey as parents, for you too will grow and develop. The first year is the time to create an enduring bond with your baby and set the foundation for positive parent–child interaction that will prevent behaviour problems later. As parents, you'll learn to think on your feet, multitask, adapt to new challenges, problem-solve and change direction in a heartbeat. At any given moment, you'll be entertainer, teacher, nurse or bodyguard.

Because babies sense our feelings and take them in, one of the greatest gifts you can give your newborn is a sense of confidence in yourself. It's my hope that this book will give you the information and support you need to relax and trust yourself more and more.

Over the first year, you will come to love and grow with your child, who will be part of your life for ever. May you treasure this precious time and the precious little one who is coming into your life.

How this book works

Babies grow quickly and their needs change dramatically over the first year, so I want this book to be as quick and easy to refer to as possible. You may want to read it cover to cover, or dip in and out depending on the stage that your baby has reached.

So Part 1 deals with everything you need to begin to ready yourself for the new arrival.

Part 2 is for when the baby is finally here, and I have broken this up into three-month segments, each of which deals with the following topics:

Parents' Journey: This section is about helping you eliminate your worries about yourself as a parent as much as possible so you can enjoy the process. I'm here to lend support for what you're feeling and thinking, to reassure you that the things that are difficult will pass, and to enable you to experience the joy of parenthood as much as possible. Here's my key message – your love is enough. In fact, it's just what your baby needs!

Just as your baby grows and changes a lot this year, so will you. Your baby will bring out qualities you never knew you had and will challenge you to develop ever more patience, maturity and humour. You'll be surprised at how your emotional development goes in stages similar to your child's: the first 3 months, 3–6 months, 6–9 months and 9–12 months. By the time a year rolls round, you'll be an old hand!

Developmental Overview: I've included this section in each age stage so that you can get a sense of your baby's growth. It's human nature to want to understand where your baby is in terms of physical, mental and social growth, and whether that's on target. You're in love with your baby, and you want to understand where he's at because you want to be able to do as much as you possibly can for him. That's fabulous. I also want you to understand that, most likely, what's happening with your baby is natural. Crying, for instance, is in the nature of infancy. The more you understand what's normal, the more you can go with the flow and stop worrying about what is or isn't happening.

Please be aware that each infant is unique and develops at her own pace, so these time frames are not cast in stone. There are tremendous variations in when babies start walking, talking, getting teeth, sleeping through the night – everything. Don't have a heart attack if your baby's two months behind. Don't compare your baby with others. It's a bad habit to start and can be extremely damaging to your child's self-esteem as she gets older. It also causes needless worry on your part.

Rather, use this information as a guide, so that you are aware of things that might have to be checked out if they are delayed more than a little. As the primary carer, you spend more time around your baby than anyone else, which is why your baby's doctor relies on your input to understand how your baby is doing. The more idea you have of general development, the better you can mentally log how your baby is progressing. And by all means if you have concerns, talk to your GP or health visitor.

Setting Firm Ground: Setting firm ground is about creating healthy routines for feeding, waking, sleeping and stimulating play, as well as dealing effectively with crying. I can't emphasise enough the importance of routines. The more you can create routines early on, the easier your life will be, not just this first year, but throughout your baby's childhood. Routines create security and stability for your baby and for you. You both feel less overwhelmed and they help you manage time well so you can do other things too.

This is not to say that you must rigidly make your baby follow a schedule – I strongly believe that being a good parent is about being able to both create routines and stay flexible. It's the middle ground – not too rigid and not too loose. This takes practice.

For instance, say your baby is now three months and usually has a nap in his cot at two o'clock. You're out having lunch with a friend. Do you have to rush home to keep to the schedule if he's drifting off in his stroller? That's too rigid. I'm not a stickler for 'must sleep at the same time in the same place every day', but it is worth following a consistent pattern of sleeping and feeding. If he's asleep in a stroller, he's on schedule, just in a different place. The aim is to put together cornerstones of a routine that you can have in place, so that you know what your 'norm' is and can work around it occasionally. Therefore each 'setting firm ground' section ends with a '**Cornerstone Routine**' that pulls together all the information you have learned.

Parentcraft: In this section, you'll learn all the tricks of the parent trade: nappy-changing, dressing, bathing, trimming nails, taking temperatures, going out. With my techniques, you'll find all of this quite easy.

Babyproofing: When we think about making our homes safe, we usually think about electrical sockets, drowning and falling. Of course we need to keep our babies safe from such hazards, but babyproofing encompasses much more – it's about creating a generally safe and healthy environment in which your baby can thrive.

As your baby progresses through his first year, your safety concerns will change, based on his growth and development. Each Babyproofing section builds upon the last, so, for instance, when I suggest fire-retardant sleepwear or not leaving your baby alone with your pet in the first three months, it applies through the whole year.

In the Babyproofing sections, I've written what I feel is best for the *overall* safety of children up to the age of one divided into age stages. To some of these you'll say, 'That's not necessary for my child because they've already learned that,' or, 'We don't actually need to have a lock there,' or, 'We feel that this particular situation is fine. Our child is so small she can't reach the stove.' That makes sense. You will need to customise my recommendations to your living situation and your particular child.

Stimulation and Explorations: Watching your child grow, change, learn and explore is one of the great joys of parenthood, and you will want to do everything you can to help him along. To help you understand what he needs from you, I give you ideas for activities that will help with your baby's physical, mental and emotional development in each range. Not only will this be great fun, but it will keep you in tune with what kinds of stimulation he needs as he grows so that the two of you can explore the world together.

Part 3 is for parents of babies in exceptional circumstances – multiple births, premature birth and other special needs, and adopted babies – in which I discuss how you might modify my advice to take your circumstances into account.

Finally, the fourth section of the book contains quick need-to-know information, from basic medical information and advice, to useful numbers, addresses and websites, so that you can have all the further resources you might need at your fingertips.

Taken together, these sections should give you all the elements you need to tackle your baby's first year with enjoyment, peace of mind and confidence.

PART 1

Before Your Baby's Born

Contents

Chapter 1

Becoming Confident Parents

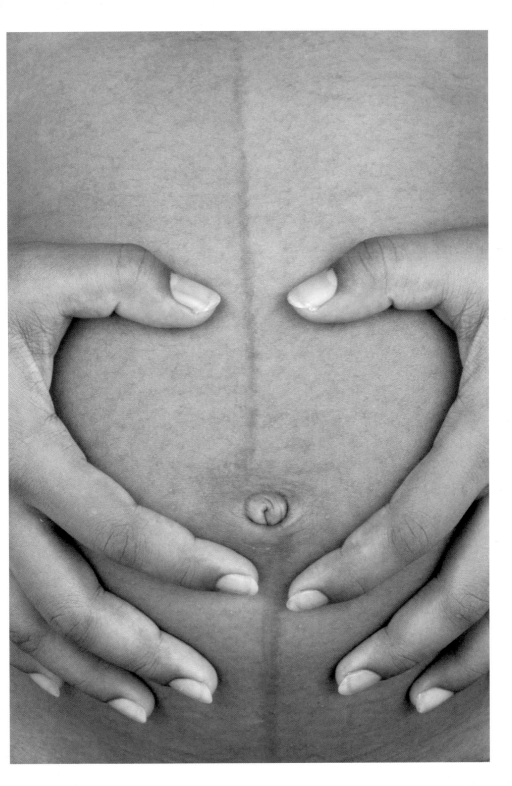

Whether this is your first child or your fifth, you're about to go on an emotional journey that is unique. As any parent of more than one child will tell you, no two babies are alike, and no two first years are alike either. You may be full of intense feelings of love, or it may take time to bond with your newborn. You may get post-natal depression or sail right through the hormone changes. You may feel exhausted and overwhelmed, or calm and joyful – or all of the above on any given day. When you speak to other parents and they say things like, 'You'll never have sex again,' 'Your house will be a mess,' understand that they're talking about their own experiences. Try not to let others' expectations get in your way. Allow your experience to be just what it is. Yours. Unique.

It's also important to understand that you may enjoy certain parts of the journey more than others, and that's okay. Each of the stages from 0–12 months will be very different and call on different skills. Some parents especially love the cuddly newborn stage; others can't wait for the more active times. Again, accept how you feel and understand that it's quite normal.

Some parents are very confident – for them, having a newborn is as easy as a brisk walk in the park. Other parents feel really scared, unsure what to expect and worried they won't be able to cope. If you're feeling confident, that's a great gift to your partner, because confidence is contagious, but if you feel vulnerable and awkward, don't be hard on yourself.

Anxious soon-to-be parents often ask me, 'How will I know whether I'm doing it right if I've never had a baby?' I always say, 'You can't – and that's fine.' You're going to find out along the way – it's on-the-job training! You'll learn that if you keep a nappy on too long, he's going to be uncomfortable and cry, so you'll change it sooner. You'll learn to read your child's facial expressions and sounds, recognising, for instance, that he's still hungry because he's crying in a particular way. As you become more intuitive, your baby will be able to tell you more and more.

Remember, every parent has to learn as they go along. Fortunately, while babies are vulnerable, they're also pretty sturdy beings. There are a few things you absolutely must do, such as support their neck, sleep them on their back, keep them out of the sun, but if you don't put the nappy on right, put the little jumper on backwards, or forget to wind him after a feed, it's not the end of the world. He'll soon let you know and you'll work it out!

Watching dads in particular, I've often noticed that the more carefully they try to hold the baby, the more she cries because she senses his insecurity. Babies pick up our energy – they have a sixth sense. That's why I stress confident care. If you're very firm and confident as you pick up the baby and support his head and neck (which you'll learn how to do later), he'll sense your competency and be calm.

But as a first-time parent, achieving that calm confidence can be very challenging. You may feel overwhelmed, which can make you nervous and maybe not so mindful, so remember – slowly, slowly, gently, gently.

Growing in confidence

I want you to learn how to make confident decisions. Confident decisions are decisions that you're happy with. Full stop.

As time goes on, your confidence will grow because you'll begin to see great results. This will help you to develop a knowingness about what this child needs, and how to balance the needs of two or three children if that's what you're learning this time. This inner knowingness comes from listening to yourself as well as to your baby, and your other children if you have them, and the more you pay attention to your inner voice, the more you'll learn to trust it.

You'll also develop more confidence as you embrace your fears. I've met women who've been incredibly successful in business and are anxious about measuring up in motherhood. I say, 'Why?' If you feel fearful, it's only an indication that you want to do your best, and that's wonderful! Any time you feel anxious, remember that it's a sign of wanting to do well, and your wanting to do well will *help* you do well. Visualise it being okay, you doing well, your baby being happy . . . Happy thoughts create happy feelings, so if you find yourself worried or scared, think of it turning out well and you'll feel better.

You'll also grow in confidence as you come to understand that when you make the 'wrong' decision, it isn't actually 'wrong', because you learn from what you did – you now know the correct way to do something. Confident parents make a decision, see what the outcome is and then decide to make a better judgement next time if it wasn't the best choice. At some point you'll have learned so much that you become very sure and very wise.

That's why being a parent second time round is easier. If you're a second- or third-time parent, you might be thinking, 'But it's been five or six years – I've forgotten everything I learned when I had my first.' Don't worry. It's all in your long-term memory, ready to move into the short-term one. As soon as the baby arrives, it triggers everything.

Parenting is about recognising that the further you go, the more you grow. There might be things you did for your first child, for instance, that you don't want to do for your second. Your opinions change, and your options too – each child's temperament requires a different approach as you work out how to gel his personality with yours and build a relationship. It's what makes your relationship with each child different from your partner's.

Thinking positively

I believe strongly in having a positive attitude because it increases the likelihood of a good outcome. Studies show that if you *expect* your baby to keep you up all night, she does. If you expect that she's going to sleep well, that happens more frequently. So expect the best and don't look for problems. That's not to say you should ignore the ones that are there; just don't go looking. And when things don't turn out as expected, deal with it without magnifying the problem with your worries. You have neither the time nor the energy.

Most women have birth worries: will it hurt too much? Will I be able to manage it? Will the baby be okay? It's just fear of the unknown. This is definitely a time to feel the fear and do it anyway, because you are going to give birth one way or another! But stay away from people who are full of negativity about giving birth. It's important to have people tell you their birthing stories, but I know women who go on the Internet and end up freaking themselves out about birthing situations. Don't borrow trouble! There's no need for drama. This is not to say that things never happen; rather, I'm encouraging you to have a positive mindset about bringing your newborn into the world. There's a lot to be said for having happy thoughts and being surrounded by people who are positive and excited so that 'happy chemicals' are released and you feel good. You have a choice whether to avoid negative people and think positively. Use that choice, full stop.

Part of being positive is focusing on what you want, not on what you don't want. For instance, second-timers often say to me, 'I don't want the older one to be jealous. I don't want them not to get along. I don't want to be overwhelmed.' Okay, I say, what do you want, and how are you going to achieve it? In the next chapter, I give you some specific ideas about this particular problem, but what is really important is that you talk together about how to get the results you want, ask yourselves how you can help them get along, then take those first steps.

Supporting one another

Because you're on a steep learning curve – whether you're parenting a newborn or integrating a newborn into your life with other children – loving support of one another is key. It's one of the things that make the difference to whether you enjoy the first year or not.

Talk about your feelings. Relish the good feelings together and be emotionally open enough with each other to express the feelings that are not so positive. If you speak about them to your partner, they won't fester and manifest in anxiety and resentment. Be there for one another; comfort one another with hugs or reassurance: 'I feel really worried, and this baby's crying is really annoying me. I've become noise-sensitive, I'm tired, and I'm irritable!' Many parents don't feel they can talk openly about their negative feelings because it's an indication that they're failing when they've only just begun. Remember that you're allowed to feel negative – it's normal. Talk about it; get your feelings out there to be dealt with. Be understanding and compassionate with yourself and with each other. Then move on to resolving the issues *together*. Although health visitors and GPs are there to answer questions, they are not living with you. If you see your partner struggling, reach out, don't ignore them.

Reaching out to others

Allow this baby to bring the family circle together. Relatives, especially grandparents, have a very special role in your new family dynamic. Hopefully they will be there not only to support the two of you but to develop a special bond with your child as well. Allow them to enjoy the experience of being grandparents by making time for them to connect with your newborn. I've seen grandparents who say, 'Thank God, it's about time!' and some who respond, 'I'm too young to be a grandparent!' How much they are involved will depend on their own circumstances. Maybe you're having a baby boy among all-girl grandkids. Already Grandad's given him a fishing rod and he's not even born yet. Or your baby is their sixth grandchild so they're pretty ho-hum about it, if excited about being the grandparents of six. Whatever is true for them, get clear between the two of you what you would like from them in terms of support and make your wishes clear. Ask them to do the same. It will change throughout the first year, but don't say anything till at least the third month unless your parents are the co-carers.

Connect with other parents as well. It's so important to hear how other parents are feeling and to share what you've learned. In the past, we lived in extended families and were given reassurance from parents, aunties, sisters and any others around us who had children. They said, 'It will be fine,' and we leaned on their reassurance to pull us through to the next stage. Now we often live so far apart that we can't rely on them on a daily basis, which is why connecting with other parents can be so helpful, mentally and emotionally.

The Internet is a good source of information to ease worries. My website (which you can find under Useful Addresses on page 263) has been very successful, and it's well worth looking at the others too. There are all sorts of wonderful groups out there. You may have connected already with people from your antenatal classes or through the National Childbirth Trust (NCT). If not, you can find a group through the NCT or other organisations listed in the back of this book.

It's important that the people surrounding you give you support and allow you to grow. I've seen some mothers and fathers surrounded by friends and relatives who are critical and judgemental, not encouraging and positive. This can be particularly problematic for new mothers at a time when you feel most vulnerable and full of self-doubt and your hormones are all over the place. Whereas before, if somebody said something negative you might think, 'No, actually I'm going to do this my way,' now you question yourself, and if you start to doubt, you leave things too open, which is not good for you or your baby. So be sure to seek support that is positive and don't be afraid to keep your distance from anyone who makes you doubt your parenting abilities. We don't want you feeling intimidated.

Let me reassure you, too. I'm the nanny on your shoulder, here not only to give you practical advice, but to nurture and support you on your journey during this first year. I'm here to empower you, to help you learn that the answers are inside you. I want you both to have that glow, that warmth that spreads inside when you feel proud about yourself as a parent.

Since I was very young, I've been drawn to babies and children and vice versa. I was the child in the swimming pool on holiday who made friends with and looked after all the other kids. I've always been strongly intuitive about babies and kids. As a nanny, I listen to my intuition, as you will learn to do, and I pay attention to what's working and what's not. That's why I get good results. Throughout these pages, I will be offering you suggestions that I know work. The success you'll achieve will increase your confidence, just as it did mine.

WHAT KIND OF PARENT DO YOU WANT TO BE?

Unfortunately, we are surrounded by the kinds of parents we don't want to be. Not all of us have been shown the best example and we need to be as conscious as possible about choosing how we're going to behave in this new role, which is why I think it's very important for soon-to-be parents to talk together about what they're aiming for.

I suggest you each sit down with a pad of paper and a pen, and fill in this sentence: 'I want to be a parent who . . .'

Here are some examples:

- understands my children.
- teaches them my values.
- loves unconditionally.
- shows them what a loving relationship is.
- accepts my children for who they are.
- has energy.
- has fun.
- is there for my children.
- is there for my children as much as my wife is.

Then compare your two lists and ask yourselves, 'How are we going to get the results we want?'

Do this exercise before going on to the next chapter, because the clearer you can be about what's important to you, the easier it will be to make the decisions you need to make before your baby's birth. Your answers will help you think about the important choices we'll be exploring.

COORDINATING YOUR PARENTING STYLES

One thing you need to understand is that each of you is going to have a unique parenting style. You create a fashion style by combining different pieces to give you individuality. Similarly, your approach to the elements in this book will give you your own unique parenting style. You may be less worried, for instance, about babyproofing with toilet-lid locks than other parents, because you understand your baby's nature and know where you do and don't need to be assertive when it comes to safety. Your particular choices make up your particular style.

While each of you is going to develop a unique style, it's important to come together and compromise about key issues, otherwise one parent can end up feeling undermined. So talk about your parenting philosophies. What about discipline, character building, raising a child who is morally and socially responsible? What will happen when you disagree? Are you both willing to enforce routines? While a lot of issues won't arise until the second year and you can't decide everything in advance, it's important to create as sound a foundation of agreement as possible right at the start. I will be giving you my advice, but ultimately *you* will need to decide what to do, and it's best if you're in general agreement, for everyone's sake.

This doesn't mean you're going to have one conversation and be done – you'll need to be checking in with one another as you go along and different situations arise – but right now, before the baby's born, I want you to learn to really communicate and work with one another, to get yourselves on the same page from the beginning. These conversations may raise issues from your own upbringing. Decide what you want to carry into your family's life and what you want to leave behind. A lot of the behaviour stuff that I've dealt with in families is a result of unexamined things they've brought from their own childhood. They begin to question their upbringing once they already have children of their own. I want you to start looking at these things *before* you have the baby so you can go into this experience with a level of maturity and awareness, and so that you do things because you know they're right, not just because.

Of course, you can't know in advance all the issues from your own past that will get triggered, but the more aware you are, the better choices you'll make. That's why it's so important that you challenge yourselves and ask one another those tough questions. You've made a decision to raise a child together in a complex society where there is all sorts of conflicting advice, and you should continue making conscious decisions together, because this is not just about having a baby. This is about taking on a responsibility and a commitment for life, and you have to stand up and be counted for it. I know you can do it – because you want to. Otherwise you wouldn't be reading this book.

SECOND-TIME WORRIES

Second-time parents have a number of concerns I've heard several times. They wonder, 'How can I possibly love another child as much as I love the child I have now?' As my mum and dad used to say, 'Of course you can – your heart just gets bigger.' You really can't know that until you experience it, but it does happen. I know my brother Matt and I grew up feeling equally loved.

Second-timers may also worry about comparing the second with the first. Comparisons are inevitable, but keep them to yourself. You don't want either child to feel you're keeping score. You'll come to love what makes each unique, especially those of you with twins (as you'll see later on).

Parents also reflect on balancing the needs of more than one child as well as their own. You have given the first one all your love, attention, praise, and suddenly that is going to be halved. Will you be able to give each one what they need? Will you have time for yourself? As with so many other worries, there's not much you can do to prepare for it – when you get there, you deal with it. Focusing on what you do well as a parent, trying not to worry and following the routines in this book will help.

Chapter 2

Making Confident First Choices

When we first met our partner, we spent time getting to know one another. We dated and talked and fell in love. At some point we made the decision to commit to one another, which is one of the biggest commitments we'll ever make in our life. Then we make a commitment to have a child together, which is the other big life commitment, and suddenly we stop talking about the important things.

I see this all the time with the families I work with. Couples discuss what kinds of holidays to take, how to decorate the house, where to go at the weekend, but they don't take the time to get on the same page as one another over crucial issues they are going to encounter about raising their child – breastfeeding, sleep schedules, discipline, daycare, grandparents, dealing with other children. Even when they focus on having a baby, it's easy for people to get absorbed in what colour the nursery's going to be and forget the fundamentals. Quite frankly, it doesn't matter what colour paint is on the wall – what really matters is parenting a happy, healthy child, and to do that, you need to make decisions as a couple.

'What really matters is parenting a happy, healthy child, and to do that, you need to make decisions as a couple.'

You need to knuckle down now and have those important conversations before the birth: what should you name your baby? What do you feel about breastfeeding? What's your take on how, as a father, you're going to be involved? What kind of help are you going to need in the first few weeks and beyond? Will Dad take paternity leave? How long is Mum going to be on maternity leave? You usually go on holiday at Christmas. Your baby is being born in September. Does that mean you'll be at home for Christmas this year? Think things through.

Of course, you can never answer every question with 100 per cent certainty, but the more you prepare in advance, the more in control you'll feel, even if things don't work out as you planned. With preparation you won't feel in such a hectic situation, and it will help stop worries playing in your head day in and day out.

In the last chapter, I talked about becoming confident parents. Part of this is understanding that confident choices are *your* choices. You should be making the best decisions you can for you and your family, not to please your in-laws, your friends or your mother, even when you feel tempted, just to keep them happy. Of course that's not to say you never listen to advice, but when you're about to have a baby, friends, family and even strangers tend to offer their pennies' worth about what you should and shouldn't do. All of this advice can be overwhelming and you can feel pressured into doing things you don't agree with. Follow your gut instinct. Thank the other person for caring and let them know you are going to do what you think is best. Take bits of advice from family, friends and other sources, and then make your own decisions.

The rest of this chapter will give you an idea of the things you should be considering, as well as my perspective on what works best. Have these conversations and plan well in advance!

THE FATHER'S ROLE

I strongly support the movement to have fathers more involved in the day-to-day care of their newborns. It's important to involve them from the very beginning for two reasons. First, so that they can begin to bond with the baby and learn how to be confident dads. Second, so that you feel you are experiencing everything together as a couple, rather than mothers feeling overwhelmed and fathers feeling alienated or pushed to the side. Mothers also need to recognise that wearing the martyr crown – thinking 'Only I can do this' – is going to lead to sleep deprivation and a loss of ability to produce breast milk.

From speaking to dads who are now 50-something and who were in their early forties when they had kids, I learned that many felt a little bit pushed to the side at the beginning and had to learn to jump in and take an active role. They grew up with the idea that 'It's the woman's job.' Many younger dads now feel comfortable from the very beginning and take an active part in creating a 50–50 partnership.

We're long past the days when childrearing was considered women's work. Get clear on Dad's role. This will influence decisions you make in this chapter about after-birth help, breastfeeding, time off and so on. As you read through the rest of the book together, stop and ask yourselves in each chapter, which one of us will take this part on? Or, who will do what when? Make it easier for yourselves later by talking it through now.

NAMING YOUR BABY

Nothing is more fun and more full of issues than coming up with a name for your baby. The most important thing is that the two of you pick something you both like. This may take a lot of discussion back and forth. Put any top candidates through Jo's Naming Test:

- How does it sound with your last name? Do the initials spell something you wouldn't want to say?
- What kind of nickname comes with this name? Kids can be pretty cruel and it will get abbreviated. (You know us Brits!)
- Can it grow with your child? Some names are great for babies but don't work as the child grows or vice versa.
- Imagine calling the name out in a crowd. Would you feel silly or pretentious?
- Is it as glam as the life you lead?

When you've finally found a name you can both agree on, you may want to keep your choice to yourselves until after the baby's born, because once you announce it to the world, you're going to hear everyone's opinion. This can definitely be a hot-button family issue.

Some parents wait until the baby's born to make their final choice. Or perhaps you'll change your

FOOD PREP

You'll want to minimise cooking and shopping duties in the first weeks, so stock up the fridge before you go to hospital – cook as many meals as you can and freeze them. You'll be happy you did so when you are back home feeling tired and can just pop one into the microwave and serve. Or get a supermarket delivery set up for when baby's born.

mind on the day. It wouldn't be the first time a baby labelled 'X' has been the ward. That's fine too.

STOPPING WORK

How much time you should take off in advance of the birth depends on your finances, your maternity and paternity leave, and Mum's medical condition. I know many women who have worked right up until the last minute due to financial concerns. I know others who have decided to take the luxury of a month off before the birth because they wanted to nest. This is something that you work out between you.

But understand that this decision might be taken out of your hands, depending on the condition of your pregnancy. If you've had a rough ride,

---

HOSPITAL BAG CHECKLIST

For You

Energy sweets for labour

5–6 pairs of plain cotton knickers to use instead of paper disposables

Nursing pads

Maternity pads

Toiletries in travel sizes

Breastfeeding bras

Front-opening nightdresses

Dressing gown

Slippers

Water spray bottle to cool you down in labour

Hairbands

Camera (and batteries)

Clean set of clothes for going home.

For the Baby

Nappies in newborn size

Cotton wool pads

Several cotton short-sleeved vest-tops

Several Babygros

Swaddle blanket

Hat

Cardigan

And remember that all hospitals require you to carry your baby in a suitable car seat to leave the hospital.

---

you might suddenly need to have an easy month because the pregnancy's becoming more and more tiresome. If you get pre-eclampsia and your blood pressure's going up and your ankles are swollen, you're putting yourself and your baby in extreme danger if you don't get off your feet. You might be ordered to have complete bed rest so you don't deliver prematurely. Under any of these circumstances, you would end up leaving before you had planned to, so be a bit prepared to deal with that.

PREPARING TO GO TO HOSPITAL

Make sure your suitcase is ready and that you've got the first set of baby clothes laundered and ready to go. I would also recommend creating a system for laundry, cleaning, shopping and other household tasks if not right now, then at least by the first month, as it will help to get you up and running again. Organise these chores so that they happen on certain days – you want to have as easy a routine as possible mapped out because you might feel overwhelmed in the first few weeks.

Make a delivery plan. Who's taking Mum to hospital? Where's Dad going to be? Who's going to mind the other kids while you're gone? What about the pets?

Have back-up plans. What if he can't make it in time? Who can you call if you can't reach the kids' minder? Do you have the number of the local taxi service? Remember, this baby may not come on schedule. And if you don't get it done now, it will get done anyway because this baby is coming!

TO BREASTFEED OR NOT?

There are important health benefits to breastfeeding. Breast milk contains the right combination of fat, protein, carbohydrates, vitamins and minerals for infants, plus antibodies which boost your baby's immune system at the time when she is most vulnerable to illnesses. It has also been shown to reduce gas and constipation. Even a few weeks of breastfeeding helps give your baby a healthy start.

There are a few other advantages too – it's free, and you don't have to mess around with bottles, powder and so on. It also burns off calories (making it easier to get back to your pre-pregnancy weight), and produces a hormone called prolactin, which creates a feeling of well-being and calm in Mum.

I definitely support breastfeeding, but not to the extent of making bottle-feeding parents feel they should be banished off the face of the earth. There are a variety of reasons why you may not be able to, including adoption, illness and certain medications. I know women who can't breastfeed because their nipples are inverted or too short. It's okay if you can't or you choose not to. Generations of babies have been bottle-fed and are just fine! Formula is now created to mimic breast milk very closely (minus the antibodies).

So don't feel badly, Mum, if for some reason you can't breastfeed or you do it only for a few weeks. It's not proof of your womanhood or of your love for your baby. And breastfeeding mums should be kind to other mums who are not. Support one another, rather than judge!

At the end of the day, whether you choose to breastfeed or not, the decision you make is fine. Parenting involves making all kinds of decisions based on *your* needs and circumstances as well as the needs of your child. I want you to make the best choices you can, without feeling pressure from others, and then stand comfortably with your choice.

You might choose, as friends of mine recently did, to pump milk from the breast and bottle-feed so that both of you can share equally in feedings. (It has the added advantage of getting your baby used to a bottle earlier – they are harder to introduce later on.) Dad can help and Mum can get more sleep; but be aware that Mum probably won't sleep at first, because when that baby cries to be fed, her breasts are probably going to go, 'Feed the baby, feed the baby, feed the baby.' They're going to feel like hot watermelons! Most likely you're going to be torn between letting your partner give that bottle and your boobs saying, 'Give me release!' So don't feel badly if it doesn't work out as you planned at first.

If you do think you might want to breastfeed, even for a short while, decide before your baby is born because she's going to be hungry and you'll want to latch her on as soon as possible to stimulate the flow.

SLEEPING ARRANGEMENTS

Work out where your baby is going to sleep. Some people have the nursery all ready – they've decked it out and only need the baby to complete the room! I would strongly suggest you hold back putting your baby in another room. She should be in with you.

In the beginning, you're going to be feeding on demand. If you can save yourself getting out of bed in the middle of the night and walking into another room by just reaching over and putting the baby on you, all the better. You'll also want to be near your baby all the time in the beginning, just to make sure he's breathing. All parents do this. You're going to be checking frequently to know he's safe: 'Let me make sure it's the same as when I last looked ten minutes ago.' I suggest that you don't put her in another room until she's at least four months old. Nearest is best.

This is particularly important if you have other children, because older children are curious. They may want to jump in to have a sleep with the baby. If the baby is by your side, you can make sure that doesn't happen and explain there will be plenty of time to do this when their sibling is older.

HELPING HANDS FOR AFTER THE BIRTH

It's important to think about this issue from two angles because your baby's needs (and yours) are more intense at the very beginning:

• What kind of support system are you going to put in place for immediately after the birth?
• If you both work outside the home, how are you going to maximise time off to spend with the baby in the first few months? (We'll look at finding help for when you go back to work on page 161.)

CALM FIRST WEEKS

Once you give birth, all your friends and relatives are going to want to come by and see the new baby. Aside from your designated helpers and your immediate family, I suggest you have people come after the first week or so if they want to stay for a while. You need time to physically recover, adjust to your newborn's needs and bond. Your baby needs time to get used to the stimulating world. Plus you would both do better without a parade of germs.

Get acquainted with one another and then invite others in. Give yourself calm and quiet. Use your answering machine. Let Dad post a baby page online to keep relatives informed and telephone calls down. If you are being bombarded with people wanting to visit, at least create 'visiting hours' so that you can confine them to a set time of day. True friends will abide by your wishes.

Let's start with the first angle. Mum, don't underestimate the emotional, physical and mental changes that occur once you give birth. It's important that you have a lot of loving support immediately afterwards. They don't call it labour for nothing! Whether you've given birth vaginally or via Caesarean, your body has just gone through an extreme ordeal and needs time and rest to mend. Some women just pop out those babies – I salute those who do! – but most women feel like they've been dragged through a hedge backwards, not to mention the hormonal shifts and possible feelings of anxiety over handling everything. You're going to need an extra pair of hands, whether it's to relieve you to take a shower, to soothe a colicky baby, cook a meal, take the toddler for a walk or listen to how you're feeling and work through what you're learning. You also want to have a lot of time in the first few days just to lie around with your baby.

Some people are lucky enough to have many people around them to give them that cushion. Others just have their partners. If you have a positive relationship, having your mum, sister, auntie or best friend as your maternity nurse is the best. Check in with them as early as possible to see if they can arrange to be there around your due date. People's lives are so complicated that the more advance notice, the better.

If that's not possible and you can afford it, having a maternity nurse or nanny is also wonderful because they have so much experience – it's what I did for many families. You can also consider an au pair or mother's helper during the day. They can't have sole responsibility for a baby or other children, but they can offer help at a lower cost than a nanny or maternity nurse. A cleaner may be a godsend for domestic chores.

You may also consider a doula. Doulas are helpers specially trained in the emotional aspects of giving birth and the transition to parenthood. Some help parents during the birth process itself; others come in afterwards to give guidance and increase your self-confidence. The Useful Addresses section on page 263 will help you find one if it seems appropriate.

Talk with your partner about the best time for Dad to be there. If it's just the two of you, can he take a few weeks off to be with you? Most likely, he's going to *want* to be around, for himself as well as Mum. Think about it together in the context of the other support you've got. If your mum or auntie is there in the beginning, then some fathers prefer to 'come in on the second week because I'm going to be bombarded with oestrogen the first week!'.

It all depends, really, on how the two of you are feeling. Tell one another the honest truth and find a way to meet both your needs, because even if her mum's coming round, she may really want you, her partner, by her side that first week. So take emotional considerations into account as well as what makes sense practically.

If you both work, you also need to think about how much time to take off. In Great Britain, there is paid paternity leave for up to two weeks and paid maternity leave for up to 39 weeks, depending on various employment conditions. Consult your employer for full details.

Some parents stretch out the time by adding their holiday allowance on to their paid leave. However you work it out, your number-one priority should be for Mum to take as much time off as possible during that first year. I know people who have stretched out parental care for the baby by one parent taking several months off and then the other. If you consider doing that, I suggest Dad takes the later months rather than the first. This gives mums an opportunity to breastfeed and be at home when the baby is tiny. When Dad takes over, she can express milk for him to do the feedings or switch to formula.

Having to go back to work and choosing to go back are very different things. If you have a choice, I believe this is not a decision that you will be able to make until after your baby's born. You might think now, 'I'm definitely going back,' and then when you've had the baby, you might think, 'No way.' In that case, find a way to go back part-time or take more time off.

Not all women have that choice. Some have to go back to work when their babies are very young. On page 161, I discuss the various childcare options that are available. In all likelihood, you won't be able to decide exactly which is best for you until a couple of months after you have had your baby. However, it is worth reading this section now and starting to look into the various options so that you are prepared well in advance.

CREATING A POSITIVE EXPERIENCE FOR OLDER CHILDREN

- Encourage them to feel part of the experience: give them small jobs to do to help the baby and plenty of praise when they do it.
- Toddlers enjoy having their own 'baby': buy them a small doll, with a box to put it to bed in, a toy bottle, miniature baby clothes, etc.
- Make the baby's arrival into a celebration for your older children: they will take their cues from your attitude and behaviour.

CREATING A POSITIVE EXPERIENCE FOR OLDER CHILDREN

Parents rightly want to make sure the experience of a new baby is positive for their other child or children. Second-timers ask me all the time about when they should tell their firstborn that Mummy's pregnant. I think it really depends on the age. If there's a five- or six-year gap between the elder child and the newborn, then you can explain a lot of what is going to happen; but remember, even kids this age don't really have a concept of time. I would leave discussing it until you're protruding right out. Of course, if he starts asking questions, then answer, 'We're having a baby. You're going to be a big brother.' Just as you should do with yourselves, emphasise the positive.

Very young children don't really understand the meaning of events like birth. Their feelings are created by noticing the response of the people around them. The more you make it a big, happy adventure that he's going to be a big brother, the more he'll respond positively and know this is a good thing.

I always advise buying a dolly with baby clothes, basket, bath and so on so he can take care of his baby while you're taking care of yours. Allow toddlers to do jobs so that they feel they're a part of what you're doing: 'Can you please get me a blanket for the baby? She needs our help.' For older children in the pre-teens – well, it's all about them chipping in too.

If your child is young, it really is about dealing with things on the hop when they happen. If there are only 18 or 20 months between the two, you're probably sitting there thinking, 'How am I going to manage two when they both need to be changed or put to bed?' I assure you that you will work it out. I actually like the idea of having children close together. In the beginning, it may give you a few more grey hairs (only joking – by now you're probably dying for a cut, colour and blow-dry), but when they get a bit older, they'll be able to be great companions for one another. During the first year, recognise that you must deal first with the needs of the baby and then your other child's. Yes, it's a juggling act, but you'll get better with practice.

You need to use your judgement as to whether your firstborn should come to hospital and see you in an unfamiliar environment with the baby by your side. It depends on what will make you more comfortable and on what kind of child he is. I've seen kids who want to climb up into the incubator, and then the parents start worrying so they sharpen their tone a bit more than they would at home. Parents, child and baby end up agitated and upset.

When I'm with a family who have just had a baby, I usually help the older ones celebrate the birth back at home by blowing up balloons and saying excitedly, 'Mummy's having a baby right now! And you're a big brother!' It's a party, a big celebration.

One thing I feel very strongly about is not offloading the elder child to Grandma's for a week because of the birth. Face up to the challenge of your new family configuration, otherwise your firstborn will feel displaced. Keep your child in his home, and bring the new baby into the situation. You may need more help in order to care for the newborn, recover physically yourself and give your elder child the attention he needs – that's fine. But have the help come to you.

In advance, think about your elder child's activities. When your child needs to go to activity classes and you've got the newborn, what are you going to do? If possible, it's great to continue to maintain the routine, but if that's not possible, don't beat yourself up. The point is that the time after the birth should be filled with the maximum of joy for you. You can start up all the groups again in a few weeks' time.

CHOOSING A DOCTOR

When it comes to picking a doctor, there is a choice of registering your baby with a private paediatrician or with your NHS doctor, the latter being free. This is, of course, primarily a financial decision, and depends on the circumstances of your family. Some choose the NHS first as everyone has an entitlement, and you have a paediatrician on hand anyway – if you have concerns, you can ask your GP to refer you to a paediatrician. Some parents speak to their local GPs' practice manager and ask to have a family doctor with a particular interest in children.

IMMUNISATIONS

Recently there has been a lot of publicity about whether to give babies certain immunisations. I feel absolutely that you must give your child all of them and on the recommended schedule.

Here's why. Despite all the news, there are no hard facts that certain immunisations cause autism or any other illness, but we do now know with 100 per cent certainty that immunisations prevent deadly childhood diseases.

We're now seeing outbreaks of measles, chickenpox, whooping cough and other diseases because people are choosing not to immunise their children. Immunisations exist to prevent your child from diseases that can cripple, that can blind, that can deform and *kill*. Protecting your child is a must. If you have any questions, see your GP.

STORING CORD BLOOD

Some parents these days are choosing to store their newborn's umbilical cord blood to be used in case she later develops certain cancers, blood or genetic disorders, or to be used for sick siblings. The science of this is new and there are no estimates on the likelihood of needing this blood. If this is something you are interested in, particularly if your family has any medical history where transplants have been required, discuss this with your doctor in good time because it must be done at the time of birth, before delivery of the placenta.

CIRCUMCISION

Circumcision is the removal of the foreskin at the top of the penis, which then exposes the tip (called the glans). Unless you're going to do it for religious reasons, in which case there is no question about it, I believe this choice needs to be an informed decision that you make with your doctor's advice.

Here are the medical facts as we currently know them.

Circumcision:

- reduces the risk of urinary tract infections
- reduces the risk of skin inflammation and a disorder called paraphimosis, which is when the foreskin gets stuck when it's first retracted
- may reduce the risk of penile cancer and sexually transmitted diseases
- may cause bleeding and minor infections, but severe damage can occur.

If you choose to do it, it's recommended that it be done in the first three days of life and only on healthy, full-term babies. (Premmies should wait until they're stable and have grown a bit.) I do know children who have had trouble with infection and had to be circumcised later in life, even as late as their teens.

In addition to medical or religious considerations, you may want to take other factors into account. For instance, maybe Daddy's not circumcised and you want your son to look similar. It's a personal choice for the two of you. As you work together to make all these different decisions, so the two of you are beginning to grow into the role of parenting: this is serious stuff, but it is also seriously exciting.

Chapter 3
Essential Equipment

When you begin to get ready to have a baby or read in magazines how much it's going to cost, you might think, 'I can't afford a baby,' or, 'Oh my word! Where are we going to find that amount of money?' No one ever said raising a child was cheap, and it's especially true in the first year, because you need a lot of special equipment that is particularly pricey.

Don't get put off. As I always tell my families, people have been having babies for centuries and you'll figure it out. That's why hand-me-downs and baby showers are so wonderful!

Despite being tempted by all kinds of cute items – and I encourage the fun of getting wrapped up in a little fluff – be practical. Your baby doesn't need that size 0–3 month adorable winter coat if she's going to be born in the summer. Remember, babies grow very quickly! And you never need as much as you think you will. After all, how many cardigans can one infant use? Unless you've got a refluxy baby, in which case you may go through quite a few. Parents often end up buying far too much. They think, 'We'd better get this, just in case.'

Be realistic. Do you really need a bottle-warmer? Know what you've got in your purse and know what you need. If you're a parent who can afford it and you want it even if you don't need it, I'm fine with that. After all, it's your choice. If you decide that you want to buy the bottle-warmer because you want the lot, then do it! Just know that a few months on you're going to be pinning up resale notices on the board at the local crèche because you've realised that some of these things are not as necessary as you imagined.

One key thing to know that affects all bedding and clothing choices is that babies can't regulate their temperature very well until they are about six months old. It's easy for them to get overheated or too cold, so it's up to you to keep the temperature right through the layering of clothes and blankets. When considering the basic layette, think about when your baby will be born because that will affect the kind and quantity of your choices.

When it comes to the big-ticket items like car seats, pushchairs, high chairs and cots, I believe in buying the best quality and making sure you can afford it, as opposed to only buying the best you can afford. That might mean saving money during your pregnancy. Whenever you can get hypoallergenic materials – mattress, sheets and so on – go for it. As an allergy sufferer, I am a big fan of hypoallergenic.

I advise having the nursery set up, with supplies in place and a packet of muslins (baby linen cloths) and a few clothes already washed in hot water and ready to go, three to four weeks before your due date. That way, even if your baby is early, you're prepared. Being ready in advance will give you a measure of reassurance, so that you're not panicking as the day approaches. It's so much easier to come home from hospital when you've got everything you need to hand. Don't open all the packages of newborn clothes, however, until after the baby is born – that way you can return them if they are too small or too large.

To help you know what's realistic, I've included in this chapter the items which, through experience, I've learned are the must-have essentials to ensure your baby's comfort and safety.

GETTING EQUIPPED

Don't be afraid to borrow things or buy them used, with one big exception: *never* use a hand-me-down car seat. This you must purchase new because of safety concerns. If you get a hand-me-down cot, be sure it meets current safety standards, and be sure to purchase a new mattress because mattresses are made with special air pockets at the front for the safety of the baby and you want one that's not worn down.

When considering other hand-me-down or second-hand items, be sure to check for durability, cleanliness and wear and tear. You want to make sure the safety features still work. Is the Velcro on the baby sling still sticky? Does the safety strap on the pushchair work? Are the handles on the Moses basket beginning to fray? That's potentially dangerous because they could break when you're carrying your baby. Are the slats on the crib close enough together so the baby can't put her head through? Make sure you know what the current safety standards are and that the used equipment matches them.

SLEEPING
Moses basket

These woven baskets are practical for keeping baby cuddled up and close by you wherever you go, as well as for the baby to sleep in during the first few months. Be sure the bottom is sturdy enough to support your baby's weight. I recommend using the basket instead of a cot until your baby can turn over or there is no longer room for him to stretch. Newborns have just come from a compact space and so they like to feel snug but not cramped.

You can buy a stand to put the basket on in the bedroom, or you can place it on the floor at your side, or at the foot of the bed if you're away from home. I prefer using the stand, but either way is fine, as long as you can't step on it or knock it over. During the day, when you move it around with you, be sure to place it on the floor, not on a table or chair.

They're usually sold with a 1-inch (2.5cm) vinyl mattress and sheet. Some come with bumpers, but I suggest removing them – there's not much room to begin with, and the basket is soft enough already – it won't cause bumps.

Cot

When your baby outgrows the Moses basket, it's time for a cot. Be sure you buy one that meets current safety standards. Practise dropping the sides to test if they're quiet and easy for you to manoeuvre. Make sure the mattress fits snugly against the sides so that baby can't wriggle under it and get wedged; make sure the bumpers fit snugly to the sides and are attached with short ties on the outside, not the inside, to prevent smothering and strangulation. When installed properly, bumpers are good in cots because they prevent your baby's legs from getting caught in the slats. Some parents buy two sets to go right round.

Baby monitor

These gadgets are a godsend, allowing you to know what's happening when you're in another room, perhaps taking a shower. Go for the mobile kind that can strap to your belt.

Consider a rechargeable. It's more expensive upfront, but will save money on batteries. Make sure it has a low-battery indicator as well as an indicator when you've gone out of range. You can buy one that monitors not only sound, but also movement and even the temperature of the room.

With modern technology, some parents are tempted to buy TV monitors. I wouldn't say not to, but if you do, use it to help you learn to distinguish the noises your child makes when she's crying: when she's really

LAUNDRY BASICS

Everything should be washed before coming in contact with your baby.

•

Babies have sensitive skin so you should always use a mild, non-biological detergent that is made especially for babies. Be sure to add Napisan to the laundry as a disinfectant.

•

Wash baby clothes separately from other laundry for the first six months.

•

Always use the hot-water cycle (80–100°) with bedding, nappies and bibs to kill bacteria and dust mites which can cause allergies. Be sure to wash bedding at least once a week.

•

Don't overfill the washer – allow enough room for the laundry to get properly rinsed.

unhappy, when she's petering out, when she makes sounds in her sleep. You want to become intuitively in tune with your baby. In the past, parents had to use their instincts to learn their baby's cries. This gadget can make it easier. Be aware, though, that if you thought you were a couch potato before, now you'll certainly become one, sitting there staring at your little one on that screen for hours.

Linens

I recommend all cotton, whether it's towelling or not. It's soft and can be washed in hot water to sterilise it. You will need a minimum of:

• three stretch-cotton fitted sheets for the Moses basket and, later, for the cot
• four flat cotton top sheets
• four cotton blankets with waffle weave that can be used for swaddling, putting your baby on the floor during the day and for sleeping under, plus a warmer blanket for winter nights. Or consider a baby sleeping bag. They're great instead of a blanket
• lots of mussies (muslins) for wiping up messes of all sorts. I had one attached to my shoulder for 17 years, like Long John Silver's parrot
• one baby washcloth and a towel with a hood.

Traditionally a new mum would be given a shawl to bring the baby home from hospital in, and that shawl would be the one that would hang over the pram or the cot. It's a wonderful tradition and hopefully you'll receive one too – or ten if you are having a baby shower!

CHANGING
Clothing

When it comes to dressing babies, winter or summer, it's all about layers. As much as possible, go for all cotton, or at least 80 per cent cotton, as this will allow the skin to breathe and prevent the baby from overheating.

Think about practicality and ease of dressing. Do the clothes have poppers or buttons? Buttoning a squirming baby can be very difficult. And do you plan to iron those little dresses? A lot of parents put their babies in fleece material because it can just be thrown into the tumble-dryer and doesn't need to be ironed. Velour and cotton Babygros wash up well time and time again and can also be put into the tumble-dryer and turned around very quickly.

Make sure the crotch opens easily for nappy-changing. Avoid clothing that is tight around the neck, arms or legs, or has ties or cords that can suffocate or entangle toes and fingers. The same goes for booties.

When buying clothes, go light on the 0–3 month sizes until you have your baby, as larger babies will very quickly grow out of them. Be aware that white will show stains that may not be bleachable; but it does look beautiful.

Here's my recommended list:

- 8–10 vests; I prefer the ones with poppers rather than ties
- 3–4 bibs
- 4–6 sleepsuits
- 4–5 pairs of socks or booties
- 5–7 day outfits like Babygros
- 2 jumpers or cardigans, 3 if it's a winter baby
- 3 cotton caps
- 1 hat with a brim all the way around for when your baby gets to three months and older
- 1 snowsuit and a pair of mittens if it's a winter baby; the fleece ones are particularly good
- 30 or 40 newborn nappies to start you off.

Nappies

Guess how many nappies your bundle of joy is going to go through before he's potty-trained? Roughly 5,000! That's a lot of poopy pants. You've basically got four choices:

- disposables
- reusable recycled cotton nappies with disposable liners
- cloth nappies that you wash yourself
- a nappy service.

Disposables are more convenient than cloth nappies, but they are more expensive and are more likely to cause nappy rash because they contain chemicals. The reusable recycled ones are best for the environment. Your local nappy service will deliver freshly laundered cotton nappies direct to

your doorstep every week and collect the soiled ones. This is a choice you as a parent should make, based on your opinion. Do you mind most about convenience? Money? The environment?

Make sure you also have a good supply of nappy sacks, those fragrant tie-handle plastic bags to put dirty nappies in when you are out.

Changing bag

Be prepared to go places with your infant. Get a nice durable bag with large pockets. There are lots of styles out there – choose one that suits both of you. Mum might find it appealing to walk around in the latest style, but Dad might not be very amused by it when it's his turn. Maybe buy a separate bag for each of you.

Make sure it always has in it:

- a waterproof changing pad
- one change of clothing from head to toe
- 3–4 nappies
- nappy wipes
- mussy wipes for cleaning up spills, faces, etc.
- nappy-rash cream
- nappy sacks for dirty nappies
- a spare dummy
- toys: a couple of soft rattles, etc.
- cotton wool

NANNY NO-NO

- **Pillows:** can cause suffocation.
- **Duvets or quilts:** can cause suffocation or overheating.
- **Super-fluffy blankets:** fluff can get in the nose and mouth and cause breathing difficulties.
- **Overloading the Moses basket with stuffed animals:** they can collect dust that causes allergies, and may be a choking or suffocation hazard.
- **Talcum powder:** particles can injure lungs. I know parents still use it, but please be aware of the facts.
- **Dirty nappies within baby's reach:** they're germy and not to be touched. Place in a closed bin.

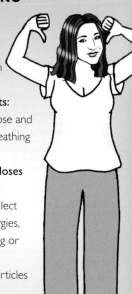

- a bottle of water, for wetting cotton wool, cleaning or mixing a bottle
- a plastic spoon.

Give it a quick check each time you go out. Be realistic about where you're going and how long you're going for, because you may be out for longer than you planned and find you've run out of nappies.

As your baby gets older, the things you place in there will change. You'll go from velour rattles to cardboard books, a milk bottle and a snack.

Changing mat

This is a plastic-covered foam pad that you put down in order to change your baby on any surface – on the floor, a bed, a table . . . You can put a towel on top of it so your baby won't feel cold on the plastic.

If you have the budget, you can also purchase a fancy changing table, but I don't recommend them as a necessity because they're expensive and babies can fall off them very easily. Also, the amount of time you can use them for is short.

But I bet you've been tempted, right? You went into the baby store and saw the cot. And the matching set of drawers. And the matching mahogany changing table. And you thought, 'Oh, let's buy all three to go nicely.' I'm convinced you will end up thinking it's a waste of money, because babies start wriggling very early on, you'll realise the drawers are too small to be of any use, and you'll give up on it by the time she hits eight months!

If you do buy a changing table, make sure you use the safety strap, and if you're changing him in any place that's off the ground, be sure everything you need is within reach so you don't have to let go of him, even for a second. If it takes the strain off your back, it's worth something!

Wardrobe

Some changing tables include drawers for clothes, but they are always too small, I've found. I suggest that instead you buy something that your child can use to store clothes in for years to come. Make sure it's heavy so it can't be pulled over by adventurous toddlers.

Essential equipment

FEEDING
If you're breastfeeding
Here's the equipment you're going to need.

• Two to four nursing bras: make sure these have wide straps to support the weight of your breasts and that the cups don't press too tightly against your nipples.
• A box of disposable breast pads (so you can experiment with finding the brand you like). Otherwise, you'll be walking around like some wild banshee with your breasts leaking all over the place.
• An electric breast pump to express milk to store for when your milk supply is low, and so Dad or others can also feed the baby to give Mum rest or a chance for time out. They are available to rent from hospital supply stores, the La Lèche League, the Association of Breastfeeding Mothers, and the National Childbirth Trust (see Useful Addresses on page 263). You can also try a hand pump, but most women find this challenging.
• Special freezer bags to store expressed milk.
• A nursing pillow, commonly called a support or V-shaped pillow. These are fabulous because they wrap around your body and really support you and the baby as she feeds.

If you're bottle-feeding or pumping

• 6–8 bent-neck bottles with the soft teats that flatten at the top like a nipple does
• a bottle brush to get all the gunk out
• a steriliser: an electric one or one to put in the microwave
• nipple cream for sore breasts.

High chair
You won't need this until your baby is around six months, so you might want to put off this purchase until then as a way of spreading out your expenses. When you do buy one, be sure it has the means to strap your baby in and use

the straps! Consider how easy it is to clean and store. Leather and hard plastic ones are easier to clean than wooden.

OUT AND ABOUT
Pram and pushchair
Before your baby can sit up well, around six months, she needs to be in a pram when going out for walks. Once she can sit up, you can switch her to a pushchair or buggy. For both of these, you want to consider durability, sturdiness and ease of use. How easy it is to fold? To carry up and down stairs if you must do that? To put the brakes on? It shouldn't have to be rocket science to take your baby for a walk.

Some parents will want the crème de la crème of prams regardless; others will go for ease. It comes down to personal taste and style as to which you'll purchase. I like to think of a pram as a shell for your baby. You want a shell that is comfortable and has enough space for your little one to lie down in.

When it comes to the pushchair, look for one that's lightweight, durable and easy to clean. Check the wheels. Some buggies only roll well on pavement and have trouble on gravel. You want one that is mobile wherever you go.

Baby sling
I swear by a sling. It allows you to be mobile and the baby to be physically connected to you. It also allows Dad to have physical closeness. Make sure it provides proper neck and head support, is made of a washable fabric, feels comfortable on you, has strong safety tabs so it can't come undone, and permits you to carry your baby facing either out or in. In the beginning, you'll want to have her facing in. As she gets older, she'll want to face out and experience the world.

There is an array of fashionable slings around these days. I say try them all and then decide. When figuring out which to buy, make sure you take into consideration your width. It's a bit like driving a car and going through barriers: you need to know how much space you plus baby in sling will take up!

Baby baths and baby seats

For newborns I love the new small plastic baths that sit on the sides of the bathtub. When you're finished, you pull the plug out and the water all pours out into the main bath. They're easy on your back, because you don't have to lean over so far; after giving birth, your back muscles may be a little bit weak. But if you can't afford one, you can always use a traditional plastic floor one. The new blow-up baths are great, practical and easy to travel with.

The reason why it's important to start off with a small bath is because in a small space with just a little water you'll gain confidence in how to hold and handle your baby. If you lose your grip, you're not subjecting your baby to the capacity and hardness of a big bath.

As your baby gets older, at six months or so, consider a bath seat. They can be used in the main bath, take up less room and give parents confidence.

And, of course, *never* leave him unattended, even for a second, no matter what bath arrangement you choose.

Car seat

Your baby *must always* be in a car seat whenever you drive anywhere. Don't penny-pinch on the car seat, and remember, *no used seats*. Any child restraint sold or supplied in the UK must now conform to the standard R44.03 or R44.04, which is denoted with the letter E in a circle and a number. (The number indicates the country giving approval – the UK is 11.) The standard applies Europe-wide and therefore European-manufactured seats fit UK laws.

Until one year of age and at least 20 lb, babies must ride rear-facing in the rear seat and at a 30–45° angle to keep their heads from falling forward. Car seats for newborns come with inserts to support the head and neck.

Don't buy the next stage on and think, 'Oh, he'll grow into it,' or, 'We'll save a little bit more money.' Buy the age- and weight-appropriate one, full stop. When you need a new one, you need a new one. When installing it, do not tip it back too far or she might come out of it in an accident. Be sure to follow the manufacturer's instructions as well as your car's manual for proper and safe installation.

When shopping for a seat, test the buckle and imagine yourself strapping a fidgeting baby into it. There are a variety of fastening arrangements – buy the kind that works best for you, but is not so easy to undo that a child can tamper with it. Britax are great.

Decide whether to get a car seat that you can also use as a carry seat inside the house or to buy a separate seat for that purpose. Either way, keep in mind that if your kid's just been sitting in a seat for a half-hour journey and he's going to be sitting in a seat again inside, perhaps in a restaurant, he will need to be taken out of the seat indoors as much as possible so he's not constantly sitting in the same bucket position.

Other equipment to consider

A large, comfortable rocking chair for yourself: do you want to buy a rocking chair so that you can feed and wind your baby comfortably and then place her back into her sleep basket? Some parents (and babies) love them; others don't. To me, it's a matter of personal preference. Another option might be a one-piece sofa large enough to sleep on.

A bouncy seat or swing: I like these because they give your baby something different to do. Babies tend to love the motion these provide. They're also great for when your baby is older as you can play alongside her. Don't overuse it as a babysitter, though.

Playpen: some people swear by them; others hate them. I believe in using them for *play* only, not for hours at a time as a babysitter or a way to confine your active baby. Overuse means neglect!

Other essentials

When someone is about to have a baby, I like to make a basket of goodies with the little things that I know parents of a newborn will need. It's meant to be carried from room to room as you need it. You can make one for yourself. Buy a basket, line it with a cloth and put in the following:

- a baby thermometer: for best accuracy, get a digital rectal thermometer – a digital thermometer under the arm can't be used on infants under three months, and is less accurate anyway

- petroleum jelly for the rectal thermometer
- olive oil for cradle cap
- Infacol for wind
- Metanium, a nappy-rash cream I swear by, Sudocrem is also popular
- unscented baby soap and shampoo
- large packages of cotton wool
- baby scissors for cutting fingernails and toenailsc
- a soft, baby hairbrush
- baby massage cream.

BABYPROOFING

Babyproofing – making your home safe for your precious infant – really begins before your baby is born with the choices you make about equipment and environment. Here's why: when babies are very young, some of the greatest dangers they face have to do with breathing. To avoid suffocation and strangulation, I've made recommendations about bedding and clothing, but making your home safe for your baby's breath goes beyond that.

Because their lungs are so tiny, babies breathe many more times a minute than adults, which means they breathe in more pollutants such as paint fumes, aerosol sprays, tobacco smoke, dust, fibres and so on that can cause inflammation and asthma. For instance, if a toxic chemical is in the air, a baby will receive twice as much exposure as an adult, so the cleaner and more non-toxic you can keep the environment, the healthier your little one's precious lungs will be.

However, this is going to raise some hard choices for you as parents in terms of money and effort before the baby comes along. I'm presenting these suggestions purely for you to discuss so that you can make informed choices. Whatever you do, plan to be sorted out four to six weeks before the baby's born so things can air properly.

- If you can afford it, consider using water-based paint in the baby's room that is low in VOCs (volatile organic compounds, like formaldehyde, that are given off as gases). The Internet is a good source for a wide range of ecofriendly paints, though you will pay a little more per gallon. Some are

100 per cent biodegradable and can be disposed of on a compost heap.

• If you have an older home (built before the 1970s) that might have lead paint around, have it checked by professionals. Dust from lead paint is extremely toxic, especially to babies' brains.

• Paint two weeks before putting any hangings, furniture or carpets in the room so that the fumes will dissipate rather than being absorbed.

• If you use wallpaper, you may want to choose one with a non-toxic finish and use non-toxic wallpaper glue. Make sure it has an anti-fungal in it to stop fungus from growing behind the paper.

• If you want window treatments, consider natural, washable fabrics and wash them frequently. Make sure they have no cords or tassels, to avoid strangulation, or buy 'breakaway tassels' that will separate if your baby gets tangled up. Never place the cot or other furniture near blinds.

• Avoid chipboard furniture (it gives off formaldehyde) or seal it with low-VOC sealer.

• Hardwood is better than carpet because carpet can collect dust. However, carpet is more cushy and warm. If you do use carpet, make sure it is tightly woven so that your baby can't pull at it and choke on carpet fluff. Make sure you air it for at least three days after it's installed before you put your baby in the room, and make sure you vacuum at least once a week to keep down dust, dust mites, and any pollutants.

• Consider using non-toxic cleaners rather than aerosol sprays such as furniture polish or air-fresheners. For all kinds of healthy products, check out www.healthy-house.co.uk.

• Install smoke detectors and carbon-monoxide detectors on every floor of your house (and have a carbon-monoxide detector by your boiler as well).

• Consider getting a cold-air humidifier. It modifies the dry air in a centrally heated house and helps especially when babies have colds, flu, or stuffy noses.

I hope that provisioning your baby will be an exciting experience. Don't be daunted. Make lists and you'll get there step by step.

PART 2
Baby's Here!

Contents

Chapter 4
Zero to Three Months

PARENTS' JOURNEY

Your baby is finally here! It might be everything you thought it would be or nothing like it at all. Because the reality of parenthood is different from any ideas you held about it, you may be surprised or even shocked by the intensity of your feelings. You may find yourself sobbing from the intense experience of being a parent, astonished at how strong your feelings of love are. Or you might feel an overpowering sense of responsibility that this tiny creature is completely dependent on you. You may feel anxious – is my baby okay? Am I doing it right? – or any of a wide array of emotions. Parents who've already had a child may be surprised by the difference in their emotions this time round. There's no predicting exactly how you will feel.

At first it can all seem rather overwhelming. Here's this little being who's exercising his lungs like an opera singer and relying on you totally for his every need and want, and he can't tell you what those needs are verbally, although he is communicating through his cry. You're constantly working out how you're going to fit everything in: do I do the laundry now or after I clean those bottles? When am I supposed to take a shower? How do I do everything else and deal with my little one?

That dependency takes some getting used to. As a nanny, I've experienced parents saying to me, 'I'm just going off to the shop with the baby to get some food for the weekend,' and they've walked out and forgotten to take the baby because they're so used to only having to worry about themselves! I must say we have both found the humour in this.

On top of everything else you're feeling, you may experience an overpowering sense of disbelief that you've actually just given birth to this little baby who's lying next to you. I love the language I see between two parents when they don't say anything, just look at each other in amazement at the miracle they've created. You're probably taking photos 24/7 and your baby's entered the world of the paparazzi. Baby albums do make me laugh – parents take hundreds of pictures of their baby at first, and now, with all the new technology, there are loads of baby movies and websites too.

Some parents find this stage difficult because there's no interaction from a newborn. Their presence is the interaction – just being there. But she's a miracle that changes day to day, week to week. Soon there will be interaction aplenty.

Try not to get too upset if you don't do all the parenting tasks to perfection. It takes a while to get the hang of baby care. There may be *Exorcist* moments when the milk comes straight back out or the poo goes flying. I've known many a new dad who doesn't realise that the poo shoots out! There they are, thinking to themselves, 'How come this baby didn't come with an apron?' These moments will make for priceless stories later on. Look for the humour because there will definitely be moments when it's either laugh or cry, hormones or not.

Whenever the baby is asleep, you may find yourself checking constantly to make sure she's okay. Then you double-check yourself to make sure that it's okay to be checking if the baby's okay. Generally this is very normal – this is your baby! – but there's a fine line beyond which you create more anxiety for yourself than necessary. This often has a lot to do with hormones as well as lack of experience and will even out over time. If you are worried about yourself, though, even just a little, talk to your doctor. It won't hurt.

BONDING

Bonding is a common worry. Parents think that they should instantly feel overwhelming connectedness to their baby, and some people do feel that. But for others, these feelings grow slowly over time as they come to know and care for their baby, so don't worry too much about how you're reacting, as long as you're not experiencing the intense darkness and real negativity of post-natal depression. (More on that later.)

Hopefully you've got at least one extra pair of hands to fetch and carry so that you can focus on giving your baby lots of love and attention. It's important to understand that there's no such thing as spoiling a baby! The more you comfort, coddle, cuddle and care for him, particularly in these early months and over the first year, the less needy and whiny he's likely to be when he's a toddler and child. Babies are totally, completely dependent. When we meet their needs swiftly and accurately, we give them the sense of security they need to become independent, confident children.

There comes a period of time where you realise, 'Oh, I've just spent two hours staring at my baby!' That's good. That's what you're supposed to be doing. In the beginning, it's all about watching your baby and bonding. You can only connect if you put in that time. That's how you get to know her, to see her body language, her little facial expressions. (You may think she's given you that first smile until you realise she's just passed wind!)

Make sure during the first month that there are lots of free moments in your day just to lie around and bond with your baby. Be realistic in your expectations of everything else. Don't get too hung up about the state of the house. Of course, there has to be cleanliness, but there's no need to be germaphobic. It doesn't mean that you don't have to take into account your other children, either, if you have them, and the realities of daily life, but this is a once-in-a-lifetime experience and the time goes quickly, so relish, relish.

MUM'S BODY-CHANGES

During the first weeks after you give birth, your body will be readjusting. Your uterus will shrink, you'll bleed heavily from the vagina as your uterus sheds its lining, the volume of blood you have will go back to pre-pregnancy volume, your hormones will fluctuate, your belly will be less firm, and your breasts will prepare to breastfeed. Your perineum may be sore, and you may experience constipation. You may feel faint or dizzy and find yourself shivering and/or sweating a lot. Oh, and that thick pregnancy hair may fall out. (Some women see this time as a new beginning and get their hair cut as a rite of passage to motherhood.) Later, when you stop breastfeeding, you may find your breasts have changed; if so, go for a fitting and get support push-up bras to leave you feeling all woman again.

Some women develop infections of the reproductive tract. Symptoms include abdominal pain, fever, vaginal discharge or difficulty urinating. See your doctor or health visitor if you're experiencing any of these.

Despite what you may have read in the tabloids, don't expect to return to your pre-pregnancy weight overnight. Women fall prey to impossible standards due to the media coverage of famous new mothers who have personal trainers and tummy tucks. How quickly you bounce back depends on your body and your age. It's not impossible, with exercise and a good healthy food plan, to make a recovery. There's no reason you can't look the way you want to. I have seen women breastfeed constantly, not because their baby needs it but because it helps them lose weight – you burn a lot of calories when you breastfeed. This is dangerous because the baby is getting more than he needs and breastfeeding is being used for the wrong reason. Be sensible and do what's right for your child as well as yourself!

RECOVERY FROM A CAESAREAN

If you've had a C-section, you will need even more downtime. You may experience greater fatigue, soreness around the incision, discomfort on urinating and gas pains in your guts, shoulders and upper chest.

Here are some tips for a speedy recovery:

• Make sure you know how to change the dressing before leaving hospital.
• Keep your incision area clean and dry, and expose it to the air.
• Be sure you get as much time lying around on the sofa as possible for the first couple of weeks. Avoid a lot of stair-climbing if you can.
• No exercising, driving or intercourse for six weeks.
• When sneezing, coughing or laughing, hold a pillow against your incision to reduce pain.
• No heavy lifting until the incision has healed. Your doctor will let you know.
• Rocking and moving around can help eliminate gas pains.
• Breastfeed in a position where your baby's legs are under your arms.

THE BABY BLUES AND POST-NATAL DEPRESSION

For most women, the hormonal and emotional changes from giving birth combined with fatigue and the newness of the experience cause what's known as the baby blues. Signs include irritability, sadness, anxiety or fear and anger.

You may experience any or all of these emotions. The blues typically come on a few days after giving birth and last for a few days, tapering off as your hormones level off and you get into a rhythm with your baby.

Lots of mothers get thrown because what is actually happening to them emotionally and chemically runs counter to their idea of how they should be feeling. You may find your mind telling you one thing while your body's screaming, 'No!' Understand that your hormones will straighten themselves out, and try to let go of expecting things to be a certain way. Enjoy things as they are as much as possible.

Dads can get their own version of the baby blues. They may suddenly start to worry about their ability to provide for the family. They may feel conflicting emotions about taking on such a huge responsibility. These worries are natural. The more you get in there and share the experience with your partner, the more comfortable with your role you're going to be.

Some women, about one in ten, have a more intense experience known as post-natal depression, which can last up to a year. It is a mental and emotional illness.

Here are the signs:

• extreme sadness, emptiness and despair
• severe feelings of inadequacy
• withdrawal from friends and family
• an inability to care for your children
• dark thoughts of harming your baby or yourself
• panic attacks, feelings of anxiety
• lethargy
• chest pains, abdominal pains or breathing problems that have no medical explanation
• drinking too much, abuse of prescription drugs
• obsessive or repetitive behaviour
• putting on a brave face.

If you are experiencing any of these symptoms, please see your doctor, midwife or health visitor. This condition can be successfully treated with anti-depressant medicine. You may also want to get counselling or other mental and occupational support (see Useful Addresses on page 263).

It helps to make yourself consciously aware of how you're feeling. Are you overly worried your baby is going to catch germs? Are you anxious over your ability to mother well? Analyse where the feelings are coming from, then ask for support from somebody who's close to you. When you bring your fears out into the open in the presence of someone who really cares about you, it can be a relief.

If someone who is close to you suggests that you might have post-natal depression, please take them seriously. And, dads, if you suspect post-natal depression in your partner, help her get help. I know relatives who were aware of what was going on but were afraid to say something.

If you do have depression, try not to beat yourself up. I'm concerned that women with post-natal depression label themselves as failures as mums right from the beginning. This is how I see it: some women get it, just like some babies get jaundice. It's *not* a failure on your part.

Do positive things to give yourself support and help yourself relax during this time. Yoga, Pilates, meditation, swimming are all things that allow us to focus on ourselves for a bit.

NURTURING YOURSELF

The first three months are all about giving your baby what she needs in order to continue to develop after her exit from the womb. You know she needs sleep, so you create an environment that allows her to be able to sleep peacefully for the amount of time she requires. And if you're breastfeeding, you make sure you eat and sleep well so that she will have the nourishment she needs.

Because your baby won't always sleep for long periods of time, you won't either. Sleep deprivation may mean you find yourself laughing and crying at the same time because you're exhausted, and that what used to matter in terms of housework or watching the telly or talking or sex doesn't matter as much any more because your priority is sleep. That's why I say if the baby's sleeping, you should be too, especially during the first month.

I'm a strong believer that mothers of newborns need nurturing as much as infants do. To nurture, you need nurturing. It makes you more able to deal with the crying and all the needs your baby has. This can be difficult because even though you've cut the physical umbilical cord, there's an invisible one too. Don't worry, it will be there no matter where you go.

Nurturing is about allowing yourself good things to eat, a relaxing environment, enjoyable creature comforts, taking an hour off to nap. How are you taking care of yourself physically? Mentally, what are you doing to keep yourself stimulated? This is a time to spoil yourself and to let others spoil you.

In the past, new mothers were surrounded by a whole group of women who nurtured them. If you're lucky enough to have that, enjoy, but because so many of us no longer have that kind of support, we have to give it to ourselves. What is it that nurtures you? What makes you go, 'Ahhhhh'? A manicure or pedicure? A massage? A nice soak? A read in bed? Think about how you can get more of those things right now. This is not being selfish. If you're going to be able to give your incredible love, care and nurturing to this other being, you've got to be receiving it yourself, too, or you'll end up an empty well. If you can't honour yourself enough to give that to yourself, then how are you going to be able to give non-stop to your baby?

Many new mums and dads tell me about an animalistic feeling of protection that arises as soon as the baby is born – a feeling that they would willingly die for this being. Rather than saying, 'I would die for you,' how about, 'I would live for you'? When you think of it that way, you're more likely to take good care of yourself because it's the responsible, natural thing to do.

DEALING WITH CRYING

In the section on Parentcraft on page 207, I'll give tips for soothing your baby. Here I want to talk about how you can deal emotionally with your baby's crying.

Tiny infants, especially if they're refluxy (when the stomach contents come back up into the gullet or mouth), cry a lot. Some babies, even if they're refluxy, can have what is know as colic – crying that lasts for at least two hours at certain times of the day (usually late evenings) and happens at least three times a week.

New parents can feel overwhelmed by that, especially when they're alone. I give you some tips for dealing with colic on page 98, but there may be times when you try everything and he's still wailing. At times you might think, 'I just want to make this baby be quiet!' You could even feel resentment or anger towards your child. No matter how bad it gets, there are certain unacceptable behaviours you must not succumb to: shaking the baby, hitting the baby or putting a pillow over the baby's mouth to quiet him.

So what can you do? One thing is to learn to inhale the cry and breathe out a sense of calm. It's like when you have toothache. If you don't get engulfed in it, you can go with the pulse until you don't actually feel the pain. Slow, deep breaths will also help you stay calm.

If that doesn't work, give yourself five minutes. Put him down in his Moses basket, go out of the room and regroup. Give yourself a chance to calm down, then go back and pick the baby up again. Make sure you go back, because you don't want her to associate any discomfort with being neglected or forgotten about. You're taking five minutes as a breather, as a pit stop, to be able to calmly pick your child up again. If after five minutes you still aren't calm, call someone – your partner, a friend, a neighbour, or one of the helplines in the Useful Addresses section on page 263.

I hear mothers say they feel guilty if they ever feel annoyed with their baby. They're exhausted, the baby starts crying and they feel guilty about their negative feelings. They're not being violent or shaking the baby, but they feel guilty just for feeling frustrated. I think that comes from a good place. You feel guilty because your baby is 100 per cent innocence and purity and you know your thoughts are not pure. Unless your feelings are impacting on the way you behave towards your baby or other people in your life, just acknowledge them and don't beat yourself up.

I strongly suggest that you join a support group of people who have all just had babies. Other people's stories create a great sense of reassurance that what you're

REACHING OUT TO OTHERS

There are lots of places you might go for advice, support, or to find other parents going through the same things as you:

• The NCT is a good starting point to find groups of other parents and local activities. Details are on page 266.

• The La Lèche League (see page 263) list meetings and support groups for breastfeeding mothers.

• Look for Baby Yoga or Baby Massage classes in your area.

• Look at the noticeboards at your baby clinic or doctor's surgery for local support groups, classes and activities that might suit you.

• There is a large community of mums online, so you can search around for a parenting website to suit you.

experiencing is normal. You can find such communities through your antenatal class, through the NCT, by meeting people at the clinic, at a music class or in the park. Go to the places where there are babies. You can also find support online at my website as well as other parenting sites. Check out the Useful Addresses section on page 263 for contact details and more suggestions. These relationships are also a great source of friends for your child. One of my best friends and I have been friends since our mothers met at a health visitor's clinic.

SUPPORT CHECK

Now that you have your baby in your arms, it's time to make sure that you've got the support you need. Your ideas before the baby arrived of what you would need and the reality now may be very different, particularly if you have a colicky baby. Would a cleaner help you feel less overwhelmed? Is there someone who could come in a few hours a week so you could nap? Don't be afraid to ask for more help if you need it.

It's particularly important that there's a unity between Mum and Dad in understanding the priority at this time, which in breastfeeding mothers is to make sure she gets enough sleep to be able to produce milk.

As I said earlier, this is no time to wear the martyr crown. Give Dad the chance to care for his own baby, to make mistakes, because then he'll truly be able to become a 50/50 parent. Some dads completely surprise themselves by being naturally great daddies; others learn 'in the field'. Either way is fine and normal.

If, Mum, you think to yourself, as your back is breaking, 'The baby will only go off to sleep if I hold her. Only I know the right way to feed her,' you're being your own worst enemy. (Well, someone had to tell you.) Eventually your partner will think, 'You're the only one who can do it, right? Then go ahead and do it!' Men can get pushed out and then women complain of not having their help. When I meet a mum like that, I say, 'Oh, here we go! Spit and polish. Polish up that crown!'

Recognise where that martyr thing is coming from. Usually it's a result of mothers needing their baby to need them, or believing that because they were the birth vessel, the mother ship, they somehow 'own' this child more than Dad. This is dangerous because their baby is being treated as a possession, rather than a living, breathing human being who needs the love and care of all the adults around her. I feel sorry for fathers in those circumstances. So, Mum, check yourself and make sure you accept all available help, particularly from your child's father.

DEALING WITH OLDER CHILDREN

As much as you need to spend time with your newborn, you both absolutely need to carve out time to be with your firstborn, together, as a family, and separately, because otherwise it feels like Mummy and/or Daddy have been taken away to Never-Never Land.

Be sensitive when introducing your newborn to your child. Don't leave them alone together, because your

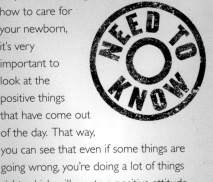

WHAT WENT RIGHT TODAY? As you are learning how to care for your newborn, it's very important to look at the positive things that have come out of the day. That way, you can see that even if some things are going wrong, you're doing a lot of things right, which will create a positive attitude that will help you and your baby. Before you fall asleep, ask yourself, 'What went right today?' It's a wonderful thing to do with your partner, too, as a way of sharing the successes of parenthood. And, remember, even if things went wrong, it's still positive because now you'll know what to do next time.

firstborn is going to want to climb into the Moses basket and have a good old peek, or try to share food or a toy with the baby. 'I love you so much, let me give you a BIG hug.' It can all be meant in the nicest of ways or not; either way, you have to curb his behaviour and teach him to be gentle.

How you respond to these incidents is incredibly important. You need not be short-tempered but use your tone of voice, if he's at least 18 months, to say, 'No. We don't touch the baby that way. We do it this way.' Then move him aside. You have to be militant in these circumstances because your baby could be in danger. It's not funny when your two-year-old decides he's going to bounce the baby by his feet. You need to teach consideration and awareness, and this will take time if the firstborn is young.

Depending on the age of the elder child, you may also find that he suddenly sees the baby as something to experiment with: 'Hum, if I do this, the baby will cry. Or I can push the baby off the sofa and watch what happens when he falls.' He might find this funny. It's important not to take this too seriously, while also protecting your infant and instructing your older one as to how to behave. It does not mean he hates his brother, just that he needs to learn how to treat him. As well as showing the elder child how to behave, give consequences for bad behaviour. It is okay to show facially that you're not happy with their actions.

Some days or weeks after the birth, the realisation kicks in for the elder child that the baby's not on sale or return. Then you may get questions like, 'When is the baby leaving?' Try not to think, 'He hates the baby!' Your firstborn is just trying to figure out where he fits into this new world. Does he still matter? It's your job to make him realise that of course he still matters, he's a very big part of the family and the birth of the new one doesn't threaten that. Your words of reassurance, your attention, will make all the difference. You may get negative words or behaviours from him, but these will tend to be very short-lived if you respond with positivity and attention. The actual moments of negativity shown by older children are usually very brief, even if at the time it feels serious.

The most common response I find with older children around their new sibling is that they remember a rattle or crib as theirs and get possessive about it: 'That's mine!' You can't dispute the fact that it was, so say, 'Yes, it was yours and we're giving it to the baby now because it's a *baby* toy and you're a big boy now.'

I don't like talk such as, 'We can't do this because of the baby. We can't do that because of the baby,' because then the older child gets the idea that the baby is a burden, stopping him from doing the things he wants. Instead, figure out whether you can or can't do something and then state, for instance, 'We have to feed the baby first because when you're a baby you have to eat very often. Then we can do what you want.' That way you're teaching your child about babies as well as how to take turns and share attention.

Don't expect your firstborn suddenly to know how to do things just because you wish he could. I see this a lot. The firstborn is used to being babied and cared for, and then suddenly, when a newborn arrives, is expected magically to know how to tie her shoes or get her dinner from the fridge and cook it. The poor child is sitting there thinking, 'You've always done everything for me. I don't know how to put the buckle through the Velcro and now you haven't got time to show me how to do it.'

Children misconstrue this as you not caring, so make sure you continue to help the firstborn so that he doesn't feel abandoned. Don't just expect him to know things you haven't yet taught him, otherwise you may notice him regressing in his development because he's figured out that it's cool to be a baby because babies get attention. This is where you ask the gods for patience, patience and more patience!

DEVELOPMENTAL OVERVIEW

Because newborns change rapidly in the first few weeks, I've divided the developmental overview of the first three months into two parts.

PHYSICAL DEVELOPMENT 1–30 DAYS

In the very beginning, your baby spends most of his time sleeping, eating and filling those nappies. And, of course, communicating (otherwise known as crying) if he needs something – food, a dry nappy, comfort, a change of scenery, a blanket on or off, to be held. There is a tremendous variation in how much newborns cry. If he has colic, it can be for many hours a day. Your baby isn't doing this to annoy or frustrate you; think of it as your baby talking to you. While he may spend 14–18 hours sleeping, in the beginning he is not able to sleep for more than two to four hours at a stretch without needing to feed. That's because his stomach is only the size of his fist!

At first, your baby may lose weight – about one-tenth of his birth weight over the first five days – although I've known bigger babies who haven't.

HAT YOU
GHT
TICE

e first month, in
ween sleeping
feeding, you
see your baby
g some of the
wing:

eflexes such as startling, rooting for the
le, and gripping on to your finger.
eginning to focus his eyes on your face.
eginning to turn his head at noises.

Weight loss is normal because babies are born with excess fluid. By about day five, he'll begin to gain so that by day ten, he'll be back to his birth weight. Growth will then go in spurts, with weight gain averaging 0.6 oz (18 g) a day and growing about 1–1.5 in (about 2.5–4 cm) the first month. Boys tend to gain a bit more weight than girls and to be slightly longer. During the first month, your baby's skull will grow faster than at any other point in his life, about 1 inch (2.5 cm) in circumference.

Any swelling of his eyelids or bruising during delivery will disappear, as will the fine hair that may have covered his head. So will his blotchy skin, which may appear blue or pink. Around week three, the umbilical cord stump should fall off. It may leave a raw patch that you need to keep clean and dry, which should disappear by week five.

By week four or so, you may notice baby acne appearing. It's a normal condition caused by hormones that crossed the placenta during birth. It's often made worse by lying in sheets laundered in harsh detergents or spit-up milk. I minimise the problem by placing a mussy under his head when he's awake and being sure to wash his face with a soft flannel or cotton wool pad dipped in tepid water once a day.

> **WHEN TO CALL THE HEALTH VISITOR OR DOCTOR**
>
> Immediately if he seems stiff, unmoving or very floppy
>
> If by week three or so you notice any of the following:
>
> • Feeds slowly and sucks poorly
> • Doesn't blink when a bright light is shone in his face
> • Doesn't respond to loud sounds
> • Lower jaw trembles constantly, even when not crying or excited

Reflexes

Babies are born with dozens of reflex responses. One is the startle or Moro reflex, which means that when he hears a loud noise or if his head isn't supported enough and tips backwards, he'll throw his arms out and might even jerk a bit. Give him a soothing cuddle and all will be well again.

Two other reflexes are rooting for a nipple and sucking when the nipple is placed in his mouth. Another is a 'walking' motion if you hold him upright. All these disappear over the first year as your baby gains control over his movements. At first, his body movements will be jerky, but by the end of the first month they will smooth out and become more coordinated. That fist will make it into his mouth. He'll begin to stretch his arms and legs, and arch his back.

The five senses

Babies this young don't focus well visually, and their eyes are very sensitive to bright light. They can make eye contact only at close range – between 8 and 12 inches (20–30 cm). Their eyes may wander or cross. They prefer black and white patterns – their colour vision isn't fully mature yet. What they love to look at above all are human faces!

By the end of the first month, his hearing is fully developed. He will be able to recognise certain sounds and may turn towards your voice. And guess what? He can even remember some of what he hears.

You'll discover that he prefers sweet smells and can recognise the smell of your breast milk. He also likes soft sensations (like cuddly blankets) and gentle touch. Babies this young don't like rough handling. You want to hold him with a confident, firm hand without a lot of sudden motions.

SOCIAL AND EMOTIONAL DEVELOPMENT 1–30 DAYS

Very young babies can get easily overstimulated. They literally don't know how to look away, for instance. If you find your baby getting cranky, it may very well be from too much stimulation. A quiet, dim room can do wonders for calming him down. You may find that he begins to comfort himself by mouthing and/or sucking his fist or fingers.

As the first month unfolds, you'll notice your baby become more alert and

WHEN TO CALL THE HEALTH VISITOR OR DOCTOR

If by three months you notice the following:

• Doesn't grasp objects
• Doesn't smile
• Doesn't follow objects with eyes
• Has crossed eyes most of the time or has trouble moving one or both eyes in all directions
• Doesn't babble
• Can't lift head while on tummy

responsive. He'll listen when you talk, look at you when you're holding him, and might even move his body to get your attention or in response to something you do. You'll find his breathing may increase as you pick him up, particularly when it's feeding time. It's his way of saying, 'Yes!'

Sometime during the first 30 days or so, you'll experience one of a parent's greatest joys: your baby's first smile. It usually happens first during sleep. He may begin to gurgle too. You'll respond with a smile and a laugh of your own, and soon there will be a wonderful dance between you of sounds and smiles. Your responses tell him that you are with him, that how he feels matters, and are the very early basis for healthy self-esteem.

Temperament

Yes, it's really true that babies come into the world with their own temperaments. Some are quiet and still, others active. Others are cranky and easily startled. Some don't take change easily, others are more laid-back and roll with whatever's going on. Some sleep a lot, others not as much. That's one of the great things about being a parent – discovering just who this tiny being is who's been entrusted to your care. You don't get to order up the baby you want; your job is to treasure the one you get. When you pay attention to the clues he drops in everything from eating to sleeping to crying, you'll begin to understand just who he is and how he bonds with you. I've come across many a midwife who is absolutely spot on with intuitively knowing the temperament of a newborn. It's true you can just tell – it's experience.

PHYSICAL DEVELOPMENT 30–90 DAYS

You're going to see such development during this time! He's going to continue to gain 1.5–2 lb (680–900 g) a month. His head will still grow more rapidly than the rest of his body. By one year, the soft spot, or fontanelle, on his head will have closed. His bones will grow quickly and he'll even develop muscles as he begins to move around more and the fat disappears.

His neck will become stronger. When placed on his tummy, he'll begin to raise his head and chest to look around. He'll be able to flex and straighten his legs intentionally, and open and close his hands. He'll become much more active, spending lots of time watching his hands move. He may turn his head from side to side. Those fingers will start to come to his mouth and he'll be able to grasp things like your hair. (This one I know much about!)

His visual range is expanding so that he can see your whole face, still his favourite toy. He'll learn how to track something moving in a half-circle in front of him, and he'll be able to see at a distance,

WHAT YOU MIGHT NOTICE

As your baby heads towards the three months mark, you may see the following:

- Beginning to raise his head when on his tummy.
- Watching his hands move.
- His own unique facial expressions.

and in colour. Eye–hand coordination begins to develop. He'll start waving his arms up and down or around. He'll begin to make babbling sounds and respond to your voice. He'll start making facial expressions like frowning and lip-pursing. Your baby is becoming social!

SOCIAL AND EMOTIONAL DEVELOPMENT 30–90 DAYS

As you spend time together, your baby's attachment to you increases immeasurably. As she gets to three months, she'll smile at the sound of your voice and when she sees your face. You may find she's more responsive to her parents than any other adults, but she will probably become increasingly interested in other children and babies. You may find her mimicking other babies' facial expressions and sounds.

She recognises your voice and is sensitive to your voice tone by now. Speak angrily around her and she'll probably cry. Talk sweetly and you'll get a smile. She's learning about your moods and personality at the same time as you're learning about hers. You may see her imitating your expressions and following your movements with her eyes. Your baby can sense so much from you.

Being able to smile as well as cry gives her another way to communicate with you, and you may find her smiling and babbling to get your attention. When you respond quickly and positively, you tell your baby that she's important to you, that she can express a need and get it satisfied, which helps in building trust now and self-esteem later on.

When you speak in response to a babble or a smile, she's beginning to learn that communication is a two-way process. Believe it or not, at this age she's beginning to learn many aspects of conversation, including voice tone, pace and taking turns speaking.

Her nervous system is developing and you'll find that she's better able to cope with frustrations than when first born. She may still have total meltdowns, but it's easier to soothe or distract her.

SUCCESSFUL HEALTH VISITS

In the first year, general reviews by a doctor or a health visitor who is a specially trained nurse happen at home in the first week, at a clinic or at home at 6–8 weeks and 8–12 months. Either before you leave the hospital or in the first few weeks of your baby's life, your baby will be given a hearing screening test to check for any possible hearing problems.

Of course, if you have concerns between visits, don't hesitate to have your baby seen by your GP. Weekly checks at the local clinic for height and weight also provide a chance to discuss any concerns and confirm you are doing well and your baby's on track, and you'll receive valuable advice you'll be grateful for.

- Be sure to register your baby with your GP with the card you were given at the local register office when you recorded his birth. If you move, don't forget to register with a new doctor as soon as possible.
- Either at hospital or when the health visitor makes the first visit, you'll receive a red child health record book to track his progress. That way, no matter where you are, you'll have the essential information to hand. There are places to record height and weight, immunisations, illnesses, and so on. The more you keep this up to date, the easier it will be to answer the doctor's or health visitor's questions during general reviews or an emergency.
- Ideally both parents should be present to ask questions and to help with dressing and undressing for the first-week visit. Then work out between you what best suits your family dynamic.
- Keep a written list of your concerns and questions so that you don't forget something.

SETTING FIRM GROUND

ROUTINES

In the beginning, your baby sleeps so much and feeds so often that, especially if you have other children, it is easier to maintain your previous routine and fit the new baby into that. After a while, however, as she becomes more alert, things are going to have to fit around the baby. Your number one priority this year is making sure that your baby's needs for sleep, food and stimulation are met, because she's totally dependent on you. That takes good time management, particularly if you've got more than one child.

I'm a big fan of keeping a baby log for the first eight weeks, and I've provided space for you to keep one on page 267. It's a way of tracking when she's sleeping and when she's awake so that you can begin to see patterns and create routines that will work for you when she's a bit older.

FEEDING

YOUR BABY'S FOOD NEEDS

Whether you breastfeed or not, breast milk or formula is all your baby needs for the first three months. Giving a baby solid foods before four months or so, when his digestive tract is not properly developed, can result in allergies and digestive problems. If he's hungry, give more breast milk or formula.

Never, never give fresh cow's milk, even if you dilute it with water. It has far too much protein for infants to absorb.

I'm in favour of demand-feeding for the first few weeks – letting your baby feed whenever he wants to. If he doesn't cry, that doesn't mean he's not hungry. In general, newborns feed as much as every 2 hours, or 8 to 10 times a day, in the beginning. If you're bottle-feeding, that's 8 to 10 bottles of 2–4 oz (55–110 ml) each. Don't worry – when his tummy grows he won't need to feed so often!

At about week four, it's time to begin to establish a feeding routine – see my suggestions on page 99. For now, I want you to record the times he feeds in the Baby Log on page 267, as this will help you formulate a routine when the time comes. Keeping a baby log is also a way to figure out whether what you're eating is causing gas – 'Oh, I had Thai last night and he's had a horrible day.'

Babies grow in spurts throughout the whole of the first year, typically at 3 weeks, 6–8 weeks, 3 months and 6 months. You'll know yours is having one because he'll suddenly be much hungrier and will feed more.

BREASTFEEDING

Guess what? Breastfeeding doesn't come naturally – at least not to many mums. Don't worry too much if it takes you a while to get the hang of it, or if you're going along just fine and then run into trouble. The more you stress, the less it's likely to work. Your community midwife is available to help night or day, and you can find her number in your red book. Other places to look for breastfeeding support include the Lèche League, the Breastfeeding Network, the NCT breastfeeding support line, or the Association of Breastfeeding Mothers. Don't be alone on this; there is a lot of help out there. Common problems include the baby not latching on properly (more on that later) and a milk supply that's out of sync with the baby's needs. It can take up to a month to establish a good routine. And if you find it too emotionally or physically exhausting, remember, bottle-feeding isn't the end of the world. But I wouldn't give up breastfeeding straight away. A baby can take both.

Nature has designed it so that your breasts will produce more milk in response to your baby sucking, so the supply should, in general, meet demand if you let your baby feed whenever she wants. Unless told by your doctor or health visitor, don't supplement with formula for at least six weeks to take advantage of this supply-and-demand effect. You most likely will produce enough, if – and it's a big if – you take good care of yourself. You can only make enough milk if you get enough sleep, eat properly and drink plenty of water and other fluids. You'll be surprised how intense your hunger and thirst will be! Breastfeeding is calorie-burning, so you need to refuel.

Stress can reduce your milk supply, so you want to create as peaceful an

FEEDING TROUBLESHOOTING

- Babies hiccup, even in the womb. If he's really hungry or upset when being fed, he tends to hiccup more. If he hiccups while being fed, just take out the nipple, wind him and wait for the hiccups to pass.
- If he falls asleep while feeding, blow gently on his face to wake him, especially if he's a premmie or underfeeding and you want to get some nourishment into him. Or put a little damp cloth over him if it's hot.
- Babies have a tendency to spit up after feeding, which can freak you out the first time if it's a lot. It's normal – their oesophagus muscle is not yet fully developed. They usually do it because they've either had too much to feed or swallowed too much air.
- If he spits up a lot, feed your baby before he's starving; wind him more often; feed in a quiet, calm place; keep a clean mussy on your shoulder to wipe up with and wear clothes you don't mind getting messy. Keep him upright straight after feeding. Put him in an infant seat to sleep. If you're bottle-feeding, make sure the hole is neither too little (too much air) nor too big (too much formula). You want a one-hole, slow teat, so he gets small amounts often. Ditto with premmies.
- Don't worry too much about spitting up unless your baby is listless, has trouble breathing, has poor weight gain, has projectile vomit or if the spit-up is green (bile) or has blood in it. If any of these symptoms are present, see a doctor immediately. He may have reflux, which is when babies become distressed during feeds and don't get proper nourishment.
- If you're bottle-feeding, every baby likes their bottle at a different temperature, so experiment to find out what yours likes.

environment as possible. That's why I recommend having lots of help and not striving for domestic perfection. You need to take care of yourself so you can feed your baby. Do what you know chills you out so that you can get enough rest. A C-section is a blessing in disguise in that it forces you to rest!

Eating for two

What you eat will make its way into your baby's body through your milk, which is why it's recommended that you avoid caffeine and alcohol, as well as prescription or over-the-counter medicines, unless prescribed by your doctor. Strong or acidic foods can make your milk smell funny and cause indigestion in your infant, or a refusal to nurse. Gassy foods, like broccoli, beans, cabbage and so on, can produce gas in your baby too. So can dairy products. These are generalisations; every baby is different. You'll find out yourself soon enough when he reacts.

I don't believe you have to eat really bland stuff just because you're breastfeeding. Here's my suggestion: eat whatever you want, and if there's a reaction in your baby, cut that food out. Or live with the consequences and know your baby's living with them too. One exception – do keep alcohol and caffeine intake low, as in none, if you can bear it. I'm not saying a glass of champagne to wet the baby's head is a no-no, but think about both of you. Your baby's brain doesn't need it!

It takes about four to six hours for something you've eaten to make its way to your milk, so take that into account when you're trying to figure out a food culprit. And don't eliminate everything at once or you won't be able to tell which food is causing the trouble.

Make sure you're getting enough calcium, iron, vitamin D, folic acid and other nutrients through sensible food choices. Go for healthy meals and snacks as much as possible – that means lots of fruits and veggies a day. You need an extra 550 calories to produce enough milk for one baby. Stay away from shark, tuna, mackerel, tilefish and swordfish, as studies show they are high in mercury and other pollutants that can find their way to your baby's brain.

Breast milk

At first, your breasts produce something called colostrum, which is a watery fluid that is sometimes yellow and contains important antibodies. It serves as a laxative to eliminate the black tarry waste in your baby's bowels called meconium that he produces before birth. At about day three, you begin to make 'transitional milk', the shift from colostrum to milk, which has less protein and antibodies than colostrum and more fat, calories and lactose (a form of sugar). In a few days more, you'll be producing mature milk, high in lactose and low in protein, which is what your baby needs to help his immature digestive system maximise calcium intake and other nutrients.

As your milk comes in, you may experience a tremendous amount of teariness, which is a result of hormone shifts. It's so common it has a name – three-day or baby blues. It may also be painful – something like the feeling of heavy, achy hotness in your breasts. Now your milk will appear thin and bluish white, particularly at the beginning of each feed. As your baby feeds, the flow will slow as the amount of fat increases. Nature designed it this way to quench a baby's thirst first and then provide more fat so he gets food and drink at each meal.

STEP-BY-STEP BREASTFEEDING
Getting in position

First, make yourself comfortable sitting in bed or in a chair. Support your back and put the V-pillow on your lap and around the bottom of your belly. If you have large breasts, take a rolled-up flannel and tuck it under the breast you'll nurse first with. Then pick up the baby and turn his head towards your

tummy, with his bottom towards your other elbow and your arm cradling his body and resting against the pillow to help you bear his weight. (see the illustration on the previous page). Bring him up to your breast rather than leaning down to him so you don't strain your back or put pressure on your incision, if you have had a C-section. You can also use the lying-down position shown.

Latching on

Place his nose opposite your nipple for accurate positioning. Allow his head to tilt back naturally as he begins to open his mouth wide with you still holding his neck for support. Squeeze a drop of colostrum or milk out of the nipple and brush his lips with the nipple and quickly bring him to your breast. His bottom lip and chin should touch your breast first. As he latches on, you should feel the let-down, a sensation like a blood-pressure cuff round your breast. It should go away within 30 seconds or so. Even if you're doing it right, your nipples may feel a bit sore until they get used to it.

When he's latched on properly, his lips form a seal and at least a third of the dark area round the nipple (the areola) will be in his mouth. He needs to suck here in order to receive milk. If he only sucks the nipple itself, he will not drain the breast well and you may end up with painful cracked nipples and a build-up of milk in the ducts, which can lead to mastitis, a painful infection. If he only has your nipple, break the suction by putting your little finger in his mouth and try again. Never try to pull him off – that will hurt. Always use your finger.

Once he's latched on, listen for sucking and swallowing noises. You've done it! This position allows your baby to breathe and feed while you support him and yourself comfortably.

Switch to the other breast when it seems like the first is drained. You can tell because the sucking and swallowing will stop. You can't judge by time very well because it varies widely from baby to baby – as little as 10 minutes or as many as 40, depending whether he's a slow or fast feeder.

Before you switch, be sure to wind him (see page 96). It's okay if he only feeds on one breast. Next time, offer the other first.

Nursing need-to-know

You'll find your baby will have his own nursing style. Some are gobblers; others are dawdlers. Some pause to sleep, then feed again. Some get frantic at the smell of the breast and have a hard time latching on. Others knead and tug at you while nursing. Then there are those who feed, throw half of it up on to you and then need to feed immediately again. Is this sounding familiar? Remember, your baby is unique. Discovering and treasuring that uniqueness is one of the joys of parenting. Yes, even having to change him several times a day as if doing a fashion show due to reflux!

LATCHING ON

It is important that the baby has a good latch. Watch out for the following signs: there should be no cracking or bleeding of your nipples; at least a third of the areola should be covered by the baby's mouth – if he is only sucking on the nipple he will not be draining the breast properly and it will also be very painful; the baby's cheeks should not be visibly sucking in and out, you should be able to see him gulping after every third suck or so.

You might discover that your baby takes to one breast over the other. If so, start him on the unfavoured breast when he's the most hungry. That way, your milk won't dry up on that side and you won't end up feeling lopsided.

If your baby latches on fine and then pulls off crying after a couple of minutes, it could be reflux, slow let-down or he's not latched on properly. Or it may be that the milk is coming too fast for him to swallow – it sounds a bit like fluid going down the wrong tube in adults. Try expressing or pumping some before he feeds. If that doesn't solve the problem, it could be something you ate, or he's got a cold and can't breathe out of his nose, or he has an earache. If you've eliminated those possibilities, it could just be a passing mood. Eventually he'll get hungry enough to eat. Get support if you have questions or concerns. Direct helplines are preferable. See the Breastfeeding resources in Useful Addresses on page 263. Don't suffer in silence! You'll get there. Sometimes babies are just a bit fussy until feeding is in full flow.

There's controversy over whether women should breastfeed in public. I think that's neither here nor there. What's important is making sure that you're in a place where you feel relaxed, so you can just go with your milk supply and breastfeed your baby. If you want to be alone, fine. Do what's comfortable for you!

If you are breastfeeding out and about, slings are great. All you have to do is adjust it so your baby's head is at your breast, latch him on and hold him with the opposite arm. You can even adjust the fabric so no one can see.

One thing that makes mothers anxious when breastfeeding is that you can't see how much milk your baby is getting. Here's how to tell all is well. After the first week, he should:

• have six to eight wet nappies a day. (Pour 2 oz, or 55 ml, of water into a nappy to get an idea of what it should feel like.)
• gain weight. (Remember, babies lose weight the first week.)
• have poop that looks like cottage cheese mixed with dark mustard.
• be alert and responsive when awake and sleep contentedly.
• not throw up too much. Bringing up a teaspoon or so of milk, known as posseting, is normal.
• stay on the breast, breathing and sucking hard, for between 10 and 40 minutes.

One common infection is mastitis. It can be treated with antibiotics and breast-feeding to clear the ducts, but will leave

---

WHEN TO CALL THE HEALTH VISITOR OR DOCTOR

Breast infections can happen and are serious. Be sure to get medical care immediately if:

• You have a fever or feel like you have the flu.
• Your breasts are hot and painfully hard (as opposed to full).
• You feel a hard lump or pain in the breast. (It may only be a clogged milk duct, which can be treated with heat and massage, but it's best to get it checked out.)
• Red patches or streaks appear on your breast.
• Your nipples are cracked and burn whenever your baby nurses. (You could have thrush.)

Keep nursing until you are seen. Stopping will actually make the infection worse.

BREAST CARE

- Make sure your hands are clean before nursing.
- Use an ice pack on your nipples before nursing. This will not only reduce pain but will help them stand up, which aids latching on.
- Avoid soap on the nipples. Wash them after nursing in a teaspoon of vinegar diluted with a cup of water to sterilise, and then air-dry to prevent cracking.
- Sore nipples? Place cool used tea bags on each for a couple of minutes. You can also dab them with a bit of breast milk.
- Leaks happen, usually in the first weeks. They can occur when you hear a baby cry, have sex, are about to feed your baby ... If it's bothersome, wear breast pads or a thick cotton bra.
- When you feel the tingle that means your milk is about to let down and it's an inappropriate time, press your breasts tightly with your arm and you may be able to avoid a leak.
- If your nipples are painful, pump milk for a day and give them a rest.
- Use a front-fastening nursing bra so it's easy to get free and feed, and never wear one with an underwire – studies have shown they contribute to blocked milk ducts.

you in tears, and your baby may get an upset tummy from the medication. The earlier you treat it with antibiotics, the less painful it will be.

PUMPING MILK

As I said earlier, I'm not opposed to pumping breast milk, because it gives mums relief and rest, particularly at the late-evening and early-morning feeds, and gives dads the chance to bond with their babies during feeding. It also gives mums the opportunity to go out once in a while on their own. I suggest beginning at around four to six weeks. Before then, unless you pump regularly, it may affect the quantity of your milk supply. After that, you may encounter resistance from your baby to an artificial nipple or he may refuse the breast. To make it easier, pump on one side while the baby is feeding on the other if you can.

Have someone other than Mum bottle-feed. It's confusing to an infant to have a bottle put in his mouth when he can smell the real deal right there.

Try it for the first time when he's really hungry. Squeeze out a couple of drops and rub them on his lips, then place the teat slowly into his mouth. If you're having trouble with him accepting it, try holding him in a different position than the one he's used to for breastfeeding. I doubt he will refuse, as young as he is, because of the survival instinct, but for older babies, weaning to a bottle takes persistence.

If you can't pump while feeding, pump at the same time each day, at least one hour after he's fed and an hour before he's likely to again, and whenever your baby doesn't drain both breasts. In the beginning, you may find the quantity is low, but gradually your breasts will start producing more to meet the increased demand. Remember this quote: 'More rest is best, for you will have more milk to ingest.'

Care and handling of pumped milk

Breast milk will last at room temperature for six hours, in the fridge for 24 hours, the freezer for two weeks, and the deep freeze for up to three months. Once you thaw it, it should be consumed within 24 hours if stored in the fridge. Do not refreeze. Store it in 2–4 oz (55–110 ml) portions in small zipper plastic bags and record the date and amount on them. To defrost, use warm, not hot, running water or you will kill the antibodies in the milk. Shake well after you put it in a bottle as the fat will have risen to the top. (Not quite gold-top milk!)

BOTTLE-FEEDING

Bottle-feeding makes it easy for Dad and others to help out round the clock. There are so many bottle types out there now! You have the choice of glass, plastic or plastic with throw-away inserts. I prefer the plastic ones because they tend to produce fewer air bubbles and are easier to clean. The inserts also prevent air bubbles, but you must squeeze the air out of them when filling.

Eliminating air bubbles is important because the trick to bottle-feeding is making sure that your baby gets enough milk without getting too much air, otherwise you'll find he gets gassy and uncomfortable. If you find gas a real problem, consider a bottle with a slow-flow tube. It minimises the amount of air your baby will get as he sucks.

When making up a bottle using formula, be sure to measure the water.

It's also really important to have the right kind of teats. The hole should be big enough to allow a few drops a second, and the teat should mimic a natural one – wide and big enough so your infant can latch on properly. Some teats come with more than one hole for small, medium and fast flow. If your baby is getting a lot of air, lower the teat size or have regular stops if he gets frustrated that it's not coming fast enough. The brown latex teats are the nearest you'll get to a nipple, but I prefer the clear ones as they are slightly firmer, it's easier to see if they're clean because they're see-through, and there is more durability with them.

Fill the scoop and level it with a straight-edged knife. It's crucial to mix the right proportions.

Tips on formula

• Formulas are either milk- or soya-based. Research has shown that soya doesn't reduce the risk of allergies (in fact many babies are allergic to soya) or colic. So choose one, and then if your baby has troubles – vomits often, has lots of diarrhoea and/or develops a red rash on his bottom or face – switch. Make sure that whatever you use is iron-fortified.

Pour powder into bottle.

• Formulas come in powders, liquid concentrates and ready to serve. Open powders stay fresh for a month if covered and stored in a cool, dry place.

Secure teat firmly and shake to mix.

Store open cans or cartons of liquids in the coldest part of the fridge and do not keep for more than 24 hours.

• Make sure you wash your hands, the counter, and the top of the can before opening.

• If you're using powder or liquid concentrate, make sure to follow directions exactly. Too much formula will create constipation and pain. Too much water and your baby will not get enough nutrients.

• When filling bottles, keep the teat and cap in the steriliser until ready to put on. Shake well to avoid lumps.

• There's no need to heat formula – room temperature is fine. If your baby prefers it warm, heat the bottle in a saucepan of water on the stove. Don't microwave – it can cause uneven heating and might burn him, it also continues to heat after it's been taken out. If you must, do it when he's at least six months old, shake well and test a few drops on your wrist to make sure it's not too hot.

STERILISING SHOULDS

Although it is said that it's okay to use a dishwasher for bottles from birth, I like to use a steriliser for at least six months as it keeps them clinically clean. Sterilisers properly used reduce the chances of sickness and diarrhoea.

• Clean the bottle equipment with hot, soapy water and rinse with hot water before sterilising.

• If you use a cold-water steriliser, leave the equipment in sterilising solution for at least 30 minutes every 24 hours. Beware that some cold-water sterilisers can cause thrush in a baby's mouth if not rinsed properly before use, so always rinse the bottles and teats after sterilising in cooled boiled water before using.

• If using a steam steriliser, make sure bottles and teats are facing down. Any bottles that are not used and left standing for more than a couple hours should be sterilised again. Be sure to rinse bottles after sterilising in cooled boiled water before using.

• After a few days, when you've figured out how many bottles he uses, make them up all at once, rather than having to do it on the spot when he's crying. It saves time and you'll feel calmer if you're prepared.

• If he doesn't finish a bottle, throw the rest away. Formula quickly breeds bacteria.

Bottle-feeding position

Sit down and cradle him in one arm. Put a V-pillow under that arm and round your body for support. Hold him at a 45° angle so his ears are higher than his mouth and his chin points out a bit. Never hold him completely flat while feeding or formula might get into his Eustachian tubes and cause an ear infection. Hold the bottle firmly with your free hand, squeeze out a couple of drops of formula and touch your baby's cheek that's closer to your body. When he turns towards you, touch his lips with the teat and slowly put it into his mouth. Make sure the tip is all the way back in his mouth and pointing up towards his palate.

To minimise wind, keep adjusting the angle of the bottle as he feeds to keep the teat full of formula. However, don't tip the bottle up more than necessary, because that will make the formula come out too fast and cause him to gulp in too much air and milk. If he takes in a lot of air, he might end up making choking noises and burping up the whole bottle. If he slows down, wind him and try again, but don't force it. Babies will get into a rhythm when feeding, to allow maximum flow and breathing without stopping.

NAPPY CHECK

Bottle-fed babies move their bowels much less frequently than breastfed babies, and their stools are usually more tan and solid. They're not constipated unless their stools are hard. Breastfed babies may go as often as they eat and have runny, grainy, mustardy-looking poo. Green stools are also common. You may hear explosive sounds. These are normal and certainly break the silence! Just keep plenty of nappies and clean clothes around. When babies begin on solid foods, their stools firm up. If you see black, white or red stools, or if they are very watery or pale, consult your doctor or health visitor. If your baby is constipated a lot or has excess diarrhoea, assess how long it's been going on for. Is it related to diet? Some parents don't follow the formula instructions properly and make too strong a bottle, which can cause constipation. Or perhaps your baby's allergic to the kind of formula you're using, causing diarrhoea. Switch to a different one.

NANNY NO-NO

Never put her down to sleep sucking a bottle – it destroys teeth, causes ear infections and can cause choking in newborns. Use a clean dummy instead.

•

Never prop a bottle up while you do something else. Always have someone hold the bottle, otherwise your baby can choke.

In the case of constipation, for immediate relief try a warm bath. If the problem persists, talk to the doctor.

WINDING

When babies feed, they take in air as well as milk or formula, which is why they have to be winded – to get rid of the air bubbles that can cause gas. Gas can also be caused in breastfeeding babies by Mum's diet. Gas is an issue because it causes pain, which can result in a howling baby.

To minimise gas pains, wind your baby in the middle of her feeding (or more often if she's particularly gassy), as well as after. I've found three methods to be particularly successful.

The first is over the shoulder (see Illustration 1). Your baby is close to upright and you gently pat his upper back.

The second is to sit him on your lap facing you and just give the tiniest twist one way and then the other to release the air pockets (see Illustration 2).

The third is to put him on his side with one hand under him, lean him over slightly and rock him (see Illustration 3). This method is particularly good if he's colicky because the pressure on his tummy is very soothing.

Giving him water just slightly warmer than tepid is also very good for getting rid of wind as it helps the air bubbles to burst. Just put *cooled boiled water* in a bottle. Make sure you give only 1–3 oz (25–85 ml) and not before he's three months. Water intoxication is a real danger and can be deadly.

I sometimes use Infacol, which is a medication that helps eliminate wind. It's a thick, creamy substance that smells of orange and which you deposit in her mouth with a dropper. Follow the directions on the packaging.

There's nothing worse than a baby howling in pain from wind. In addition to winding position 3, try massaging his

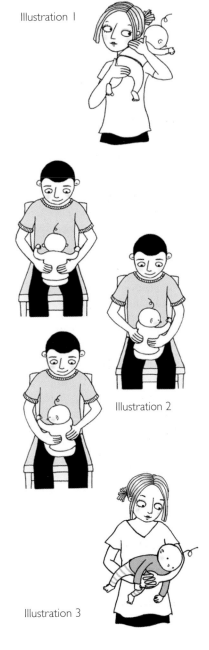

Illustration 1

Illustration 2

Illustration 3

97

tummy and giving him a warm bath, and, as much as you can, distract him with some kind of calm stimulation. Some babies have favourite songs that do the trick. Singing and rocking can help. When a baby's in pain, it's awful because he's so helpless and you're so helpless. Ride with it, knowing it will end.

When he's older, there are some other medical aids you can try, like gripe water, which you put into his mouth 20 minutes before you feed him. This can really stop the build-up of air bubbles. Please check on the back of the bottle for the proper ages and instructions.

COLIC

I have already talked a little about colic – crying which lasts for at least two hours a day at least three days a week. It begins in the first month. It was thought to be caused by gas, but some medical experts now think it's the result of an immature nervous system that is easily irritated. Try the winding remedies suggested above. If that doesn't work:

- put him next to a vibrating machine like a tumble-dryer.
- take him for a ride in the car.
- try repetitive rocking movements.
- carry him tight across your body.
- give him a dummy to suck.
- dance with him.
- experiment with various music to find a song that works.
- take turns with your partner.

I promise you he'll grow out of it, usually around the fourth month, which is hard to remember when he's been wailing for four hours. Whatever you do, remember, don't shake him in frustration. It can cause brain damage or death. If you're losing control, take a break. If no one is there, put him down in his Moses basket and go into another room. Call a friend or a hotline and talk about how you're feeling until you're calm again.

If you have a colicky baby, be sure to line up lots of help – spouse, friends, relatives. There are helplines listed in the Support and Advice portion of the

Useful Addresses on page 266. Constant crying is not something one person should endure by herself! It can bring you and your partner to desperation. But you can only do what you can do, and as long as your baby has you to hold him, he has his parents' love while this is happening, which is a very good thing.

ESTABLISHING A FEEDING ROUTINE

At about week four, you can begin to establish a feeding routine. It's important to do this because otherwise your baby can overfeed, whether breast- or bottle-fed. Because babies suck for comfort as well as hunger, if you offer food every time they cry, they can end up eating too much and becoming more refluxy as a way of dealing with too much food. You don't have to worry that he's not getting enough food as long as he's continuing to gain weight. You'll know that by your weekly weigh-ins. To reassure yourself, write the results down in his health record book. He should also be wetting 6–8 nappies per day.

Here's how you create a routine. You've been tracking when your baby's been eating and sleeping in the baby log. Now you can see that your baby ate, fell asleep, woke up after a couple hours and wanted to feed. That means he can go a couple of hours without a feed: he's grown, his tummy can hold more food at a time. In the beginning, it was probably only 2 oz (55 ml); now he can take 4 oz (110 ml) or so and that will last him longer. So you take those two hours and stretch them out a bit – feed him at two and a quarter hours, say, or two and a half. Try a dummy, to see if he will suck on that for a while to keep him going.

You need to keep stretching out the time to move on from on-demand feeding to feeding every two hours to three hours (four hours for bottle-fed), unless your baby is very refluxy, in which case you want to do more frequent, small feedings.

As he gets older, he can take more milk at each feeding and therefore last longer. At six to eight weeks, if bottle-feeding, add 1 oz (25 ml), and if it goes down, he should hold out for four hours as shown in the cornerstone routine for 6 weeks to 3 months on page 110. Over the three months, bottle-feeders should go from ten bottles of 2–4 oz (55–110 ml) at birth to six bottles of 4–5 oz (110–140 ml) and then to five bottles of 5–6 oz (140–170 ml).

If breastfeeding, you have to measure by time to gauge how much your baby is getting because you can't see what he's taking in. At six to eight weeks, increase the time by ten minutes. As time goes on, increase again. Eventually, you'll start to recognise that your baby's intake will increase as he gets older.

He's able to take in more faster and you'll be able to judge that he's had a proper intake of food in a shorter time. You'll feel the sense of emptiness, like 'he's had a good feed'. It's kind of like having a baby on a bottle who goes from a slow-flow teat to a fast-flow one. So you may sense that he's getting enough in 20 minutes where it used to be 30 or 40.

Disruptions

If your baby's sick – has a fever, thrush, an infection – it's important that he stays hydrated, but he may be off his food, especially with thrush, which is painful. At these times, you need to recognise that the routine's out the window – your baby needs more frequent feedings so he stays hydrated and doesn't lose weight.

Teething and growth spurts or travel to other time zones also disrupt a routine. Both eating and sleeping can be affected. Do the best you can and re-establish a routine as soon as possible.

SLEEPING

One of the main developmental tasks of the first year is to sleep. That's because the proper amount of sleep is critical to healthy physical and mental development. The National Sleep Foundation recommends 10.5–18 hours of sleep per day for infants up to three months, and I agree, so you should be doing all you can to make that easy – and safe. There are a number of things you can do to reduce the risk of Sudden Infant Death Syndrome (SIDS):

- Always put him to sleep on his back on firm bedding to reduce the possibility of choking. Babies who sleep on their tummies have a 21 times higher risk of SIDS.
- Place your baby with his feet towards the foot of the cot or pram,

to prevent him wriggling down under the covers, and make the covers up so that they reach no higher than his chest. Covers should be securely tucked in so they can't slip over the baby's head.

• Don't let your baby get too hot (or cold). The ideal temperature in a baby's room is 64 °F (18°C).

• Don't smoke in the same room as your baby.

• It's best to keep your baby's cot in your room for at least the first four months. While it's lovely to have your baby with you for a cuddle or a feed, always put your baby back in his cot before you go to sleep as there is a link between sharing a bed, sofa or armchair for sleeping and cot death.

See the illustrations for two safe sleeping positions – flat on the back or one shoulder elevated, which works for a very refluxy baby.

During the first three months, it's really not necessary to have your baby sleeping in a bedroom when he takes those naps, although it's good practice for you. If he falls asleep in his bouncing seat, fair enough. It's important for

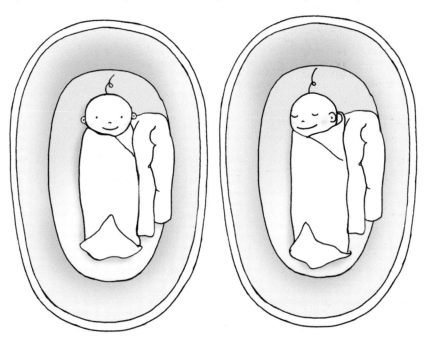

your baby to fall asleep listening to house noises around him to get him used to a certain amount of noise while sleeping. I'm not suggesting that as soon as your baby falls off to sleep you put the vacuum cleaner on, but you don't have to have complete silence. You want a resilient, adaptable baby who doesn't have to have his own room, a blackout blind and total quiet to fall asleep. That tends to create a baby who may have trouble going to sleep in other settings.

If you are using a cot straight away, ensure that you make up only the bottom half of the cot, with the blankets reaching just up to your baby's tummy and no higher. If you put him at the top, he can wriggle down and suffocate. At the bottom, he's got nowhere to go. Also, never use quilts or duvets in either the Moses basket or the cot. Babies can get caught underneath them and it could be fatal.

Medical experts don't recommend sleeping with infants as you can accidentally roll over in your sleep and suffocate them. Also, your body heat can cause them to get overheated. I discourage infants regularly sleeping in

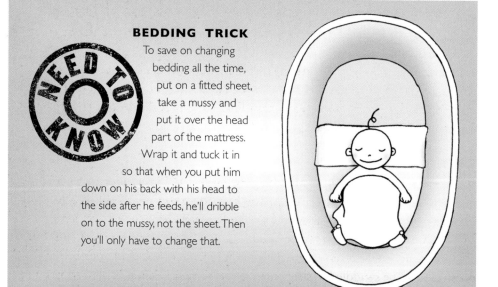

BEDDING TRICK

To save on changing bedding all the time, put on a fitted sheet, take a mussy and put it over the head part of the mattress. Wrap it and tuck it in so that when you put him down on his back with his head to the side after he feeds, he'll dribble on to the mussy, not the sheet. Then you'll only have to change that.

your bed because you're creating a habit that will cause you no end of grief later on. As a nanny, I've had to troubleshoot many toddlers who are so used to sleeping in their parents' bed that they know no different. Getting them off to sleep in their own bed has become a real problem. I want you to create good sleeping habits from the beginning.

> 'No matter how many times he cries during this period, you need to offer food and check the nappy.'

Whether he sleeps in his Moses basket in your room or his own, don't expect your baby to sleep through the night consistently until he's on solid foods. A lot of mothers say, 'My four-week-old is sleeping through the night,' but you will very probably find that it's not consistent – one week on and then one week off again. His tummy just gets empty too fast. As your infant reaches the three-month mark, he may take a late feed at midnight and sleep right the way through to the morning. Hallelujah! That means you get a good night's sleep too! But that is not likely to happen consistently until solids are introduced.

This is not yet the time to create a firm bedtime policy – your baby would probably be crying for lack of food. No matter how many times he cries during this period, you need to offer food and check the nappy. It's only four months or so to get through.

SWADDLING

When your baby is newborn, swaddling him will help him feel secure since he's been so tightly compacted in the womb. I like to swaddle a baby to help him go to sleep, but when a baby is awake, it's important for him to have space and to be able to kick his feet around and see where his toes and hands are, unless he's very irritable without wrapping. And if you find your baby doesn't like to be swaddled to sleep, don't do it. You can experiment by trying it each way for a few days and see which works best.

Zero to three months

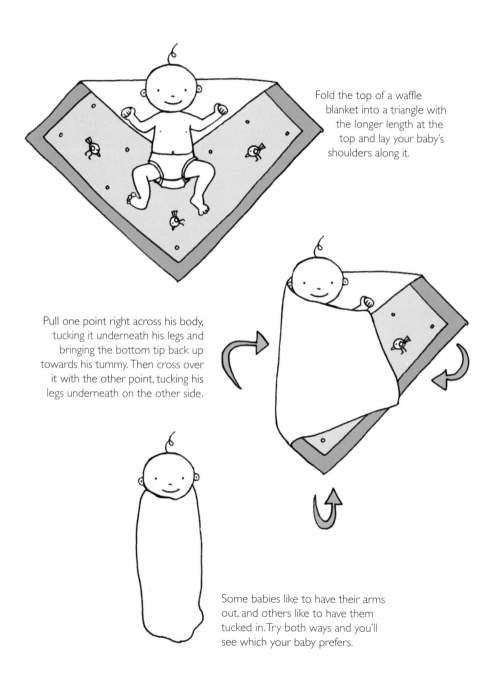

Fold the top of a waffle blanket into a triangle with the longer length at the top and lay your baby's shoulders along it.

Pull one point right across his body, tucking it underneath his legs and bringing the bottom tip back up towards his tummy. Then cross over it with the other point, tucking his legs underneath on the other side.

Some babies like to have their arms out, and others like to have them tucked in. Try both ways and you'll see which your baby prefers.

To swaddle, fold up a waffle blanket into a triangle shape with the longer length at the top, lay your baby's shoulders along it and then very neatly pull one point right across his body in an angular way, tucking it underneath his legs and bringing the bottom tip back up towards his tummy. Then cross over it with the other point and tuck it underneath the legs on the other side. (See the illustrations on the opposite page.) Some babies like to have their arms out, and others like to have them tucked in. Try it both ways and you'll see which your baby prefers.

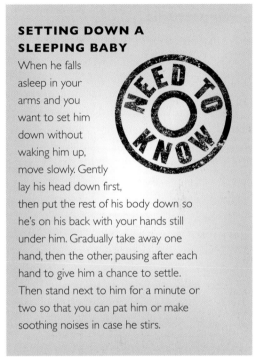

SETTING DOWN A SLEEPING BABY

When he falls asleep in your arms and you want to set him down without waking him up, move slowly. Gently lay his head down first, then put the rest of his body down so he's on his back with your hands still under him. Gradually take away one hand, then the other, pausing after each hand to give him a chance to settle. Then stand next to him for a minute or two so that you can pat him or make soothing noises in case he stirs.

Remember, however, to be careful not to overheat your baby. Make sure the room is not overheated as well. You want to be able to take the chill off the room without drying it out too much. If the room is very dry and stuffy from central heating, place some water bowls on top of the radiators to moisten the air, or get a humidifier.

GETTING BABY OFF TO SLEEP

Many babies fall asleep to a musical mobile hanging over the Moses basket or cot, and that's fine. I've found, however, that in the beginning nothing beats rocking, babe in arms. You'll find you make up your own tune and move according to that. It's the repetition that works, but make sure you're not making your baby or yourself dizzy by swinging around like the teacups at Disneyland Paris. Gently! And sing softly. This is about going to sleep, not revving up.

Sleep patterns

Every baby is different. I'm going to show you one baby's sleeping pattern from newborn to four weeks to give you a rough idea of what you might expect. But remember no two babies are alike.

Until your baby is feeding every two to four hours, there is no consistancy. It's all new and you just need to feel your way. Don't panic if it takes a few weeks to get into a routine.

> **AN EXAMPLE OF A SLEEP ROUTINE 0–4 WEEKS**
>
> Your baby may wake on a rolling schedule of every 2–3 hours, generally waking for food. Once the baby has fed and winded, take the opportunity to change his nappy and make sure he is comfortable and warm, and by this time he will probably be ready to settle off to sleep again. Remember that no two babies are alike, and at this stage you should feed them as often as they seem hungry.
>
> This pattern will repeat itself over a 24-hour period, though some babies may start to sleep for slightly longer periods at night. However, day or night, do not let your baby go for more than four hours without a feed.

MY DUMMY PHILOSOPHY

I like to give a newborn a dummy when he goes to sleep. Here's why: a baby's instinct is to suck and then fall asleep. If you give him something to suck on, he'll fall asleep more easily because of the association. So a dummy is a sleep aid. However, not every baby likes a dummy, so check it out and see.

As babies become older, that pacifier becomes something that they literally take into their own hands to soothe themselves, so it has a use as a sleep aid and for self-soothing.

Unfortunately, dummies are often misused by parents when their baby is awake to stop him from making noise so they don't have to think about what he might need for stimulation or comfort. They are also used for too long. No baby should go past a year with a dummy, and the sooner he can sleep without one, the better. Overuse of dummies can stop a child from learning other ways to comfort himself. It also arches the mouth and can cause mouth sores and buck teeth, and delay speech. So wean it away at no later than 12 months during the day, and 18 months at night.

If you use a dummy, make sure it's kept clean because it can obviously collect a lot of germs. Wash it out by hand with lukewarm water and very mild soap and rinse thoroughly. If you put it in the dishwasher or the steriliser, the rubber becomes scalded.

LEARNING YOUR BABY'S CRIES

Crying is how babies communicate when they're hungry, tired, afraid, bored, frustrated, overwhelmed, wet, cold, hot, in pain . . . Life outside the womb is stressful, and it takes a while for a newborn to adjust to it. Soon he'll get used to life in the big, exciting world and be less stressed, and you'll get better at understanding and meeting his needs.

Work out why your baby's crying. What does that cry mean? And the tone within that cry? Is it sporadic? What's the pitch? Pay attention and you'll develop an

DEALING WITH CRYING NEWBORNS

One of these suggestions will work, unless he's poorly:

• Check the nappy first and then offer food.
• If he's dry and full, try movement: walking, rocking, jiggling, swaying, patting.
• Put him close to your heart. He's used to hearing that in the womb.
• Sing or hum softly or turn on soothing music. Experiment to see which works best. Your voice, because he's heard it in the womb, is often best, especially with lots of tiny kisses.
• Try white noise – a tumble-dryer, vacuum or one of those fancy white-noise machines.
• See if swaddling helps.
• Put him in his seat or gym: maybe he's bored.
• Have your partner try.

intuitive knowingness: 'Oh, that's because he's hungry. The last time he fed was two hours ago, and I've just changed the nappy . . .' There is what I call an elimination period, when you go through all the things it can't be, and the more you do it, the quicker your brain becomes at checking things off.

When babies are young, they are not crying to manipulate, irritate, or annoy you as they might in toddlerhood (which is when I suggest active ignoring in certain circumstances). Babies are simply trying to express a real need, and so you should try, as much as possible, to figure out and respond to that need. Some babies have very sensitive nervous systems – what they're communicating is 'Ouch', and there may not be much you can do. The more you pay attention, the more you'll learn what your baby's cries mean.

Some babies cry until they gag. They might be having a temper tantrum, which has escalated to a point where the baby doesn't even know why he's crying, and that may cause a spasm – hence the gagging. Just clean up the mess and try to calm him down as best as possible.

PARENTCRAFT

In this section, you'll learn all the tricks of the parent trade: nappy-changing, dressing, bathing, trimming nails, taking temperatures, going out. With my techniques, you'll find all of this quite easy.

HOLDING AND CARRYING

Yes, your baby is a tiny, vulnerable being, but the good news is that he's a lot sturdier than you might imagine. He's not made of glass. In fact, the more gently yet firmly you hold and carry him, the more secure he will feel and the happier he will be.

You probably already know that his neck needs to be supported. It's because his head is very big in comparison to the rest of his body, which makes it wobbly. Parents going for a kiss have been known to end up with a shiner if they're not careful.

A good basic holding and carrying position is to have one hand supporting his head and neck, and the other his upper legs and bottom. Use it to pick him up or set him down, to carry him over one shoulder, to nurse or bottle-feed. That way, he won't feel like he's falling, which may set off the startle reflex – a flailing of arms and legs that can startle both of you.

One of the key tasks of baby's first year is to bond strongly with his caregivers. It's the basis for his ability to bond later in life with other loved ones. Physical closeness, touching, cuddling – these are all ways to promote this crucial attachment. Closeness allows your baby to feel safe and creates the intimacy that shows him he's loved and cared for. Holding and carrying help create bonding as well as a sense of safety that will keep the crying down. A baby held is a baby content. This usually isn't hard because all you want to do is cuddle him anyway! But because babies can't regulate their temperatures when they're first born, she may get very hot from your body heat, so be sure to put her down every now and again, for her sake as well as yours. My carrying recommendation doesn't mean you have to hold her 24/7. You've got things to do, if it's only going to the bathroom. It's better, for instance, for your baby to be put down where she can see you than to be attached to your hip when you're trying to cook. That's dangerous!

When you have to lay your baby down, or sit your baby up, as much as possible keep him in eyeshot because he's very tiny. It makes him frightened if he doesn't know where you are. Give him something to distract himself with. Put one of those baby gyms over his seat or Moses basket. He'll get used to seeing you from a distance and being able to play as well.

If you have to go from one room to the next, talk. 'Hello, baby! It's okay. Mummy's coming back!' There's something very valuable in the fact that every time he doesn't see you and then sees you again, he learns you've come back. It's like peek-a-boo, isn't it? Eventually babies understand that just because you're not in the room, it doesn't mean you're not there. And that helps them feel secure.

When it comes to holding and carrying, I'm talking to dads, grandparents, aunts too. For fathers, holding and carrying your baby is a chance to really connect. Perhaps the last time you held something with purpose was that football or rugby ball a few Sundays ago playing with your friends in the park. Now you get to hold your baby and talk shop. For some dads, it's easy, and for others, it's a little difficult at first as they feel very big in comparison and scared to hold a young one that's so new! But the more you practise, the more comfortable you'll become. Whether you're a CEO or not, you're a star in your baby's life and he needs all your love and care as well as Mum's.

A friend of mine who had just had a baby boy couldn't wait to put him in the latest car seat, latest bouncer, latest stroller – he embraced all the equipment for his little one from the start. When I laughed about it, he replied, 'Hey ho, he's a man's man and you know us guys like gadgets! I'm starting him early!'

CORNERSTONE ROUTINE 4–6 WEEKS

This routine is based on a baby who feeds roughly every 3 hours. If your baby finds it hard to go for this long before feeling hungry you should increase the frequency and adapt the routine accordingly. Time all feeds from when your baby begins to feed.

7am	Breastfeed 30–40 minutes or bottle-feed 2–4 oz (55–110 ml)	Once you have finished feeding, winding, changing and settling the baby, don't forget to look after yourself! Make sure you eat a good breakfast, and if you can, try to grab some sleep while the baby sleeps.
10am	Breastfeed 30–40 minutes or bottle-feed 2–4 oz (55–110 ml)	Once you have fed, winded and changed the baby, he may be sleepy, or he may want to have some awake time on his playmat or on your lap. While this will be fun, don't try to keep him awake for too long: he will need another sleep before lunch. It is also vital that in good time before the baby's next feed you have eaten a good meal yourself. That way, you will be relaxed enough to give your baby a good meal. If you are breastfeeding, make sure you drink a lot of liquids – you need at least 6–8 glasses of liquid per day.
1pm	Breastfeed 30–40 minutes or bottle-feed 2–4 oz (55–110 ml)	After lunch, you may find it useful to settle the baby back to sleep in his pram (make sure it is suitable for a newborn baby and lies completely flat) rather than his Moses basket, as this can be a good chance to go for a walk, meet friends, run errands, or if necessary collect other children from nursery or school.
4pm	Breastfeed 30–40 minutes or bottle-feed 2–4 oz (55–110 ml)	Make sure you have a good snack just before or during this feed as you want to be able to provide enough energy for the evening routine and 7 o'clock feed.

7pm	Breastfeed 30–40 minutes or bottle-feed 2–4 oz (55–110 ml)	About an hour before this feed, you might want to bath your baby, and get him into night-time clothes. After you have fed, winded and changed his nappy, settle the baby into his Moses basket or cot for the night. Try to use the time in between now and the next feed to unwind – eat a good meal, talk to your partner, or perhaps have a relaxing bath. If you have decided to start expressing, make sure that you do so at least an hour before the next feed to give your milk supply a chance to replenish sufficiently.
10pm	Breastfeed 30–40 minutes or bottle-feed 2–4 oz (55–110 ml)	If you want to start expressing, and letting your partner take over one feed, discuss whether you would prefer to make it this feed or the midnight one. Either way, make sure you get some sleep while he does it.
12am	Breastfeed 30–40 minutes or bottle-feed 2–4 oz (55–110 ml)	Once you have fed, winded, changed and settled the baby for the night, make sure that everything is laid out ready for feeding and changing the baby in the night, and place a jug of water next to your bed.
3 or 4am	Breastfeed 30–40 minutes or bottle-feed 2–4 oz (55–110 ml)	Your baby will probably wake for a feed at some time in the small hours – you need to offer him food as well as checking he is properly winded and dry every time he wakes at this age. No matter how tempting it is to feed him quickly and go straight back to sleep afterwards, make sure you wind him thoroughly, change him and settle him back into his own Moses basket or cot. It will pay off with just that bit extra sleep in the morning.

CORNERSTONE ROUTINE 6 WEEKS–3 MONTHS

If your baby is feeding well and gaining weight, you can try stretching out the feeds a little by feeding a bit more at each meal. By the three-month mark you should have increased the feeds to 5–6 oz (140–170 ml) for bottle-fed babies. A breastfed baby should also be getting more milk, but you may find that she is able to take the milk more quickly, so don't be alarmed if she feeds for a slightly shorter time – say 20–30 minutes – so long as you feel she has drained the breast thoroughly, and she continues to gain weight and fill nappies. At the beginning of this period your baby will still need at least six feeds a day, with perhaps one night feed. If she can take on more milk at each feed, by three months she may be down to five feeds a day with a night feed if necessary. Time all feeds from when your baby begins to feed.

7am	Breastfeed 30–40 minutes or bottle-feed 4–5 oz (110–140 ml)	Make sure you try and increase the volume of all this and all the day's feeds as the weeks go by. Once you have fed the baby, winded her, and given her a small amount of morning conversation, she will probably be ready to sleep again. Make sure you feed yourself at this point.
10am	Breastfeed 30–40 minutes or bottle-feed 4–5 oz (110–140 ml)	As the baby gets older, you will find that she doesn't need to settle straight back down to sleep after each feed. You may well find that your local baby groups, or classes such as baby massage, take place mid-morning, so there is a good opportunity to take her to these after this feed. But make sure she napped well in the morning or neither of you will enjoy them thoroughly! Afterwards, she will still need another good sleep to carry her through until lunchtime.

Time	Feed	Notes
2pm	Breastfeed 30–40 minutes or bottle-feed 4–5 oz (110–140 ml)	Give yourself a good lunch in time to be relaxed and ready for this feed. After feeding, winding and changing, your baby might enjoy a bit of tummy time or other stimulation, but make sure that she also gets a good long nap in the afternoon.
5.30pm	Breastfeed 30–40 minutes or bottle-feed 4–5 oz (110–140 ml)	As the weeks go by, you might find that you can give this feed a bit later, in preparation for dropping one of the day's feeds. But don't force it if the baby is hungry. Prepare her for bed beforehand, and get into the habit of reading her a story or singing her a special song before putting her down to sleep.
8.30pm	Breastfeed 30–40 minutes or bottle-feed 4–5 oz (110–140 ml)	If the baby is not too hungry and you have managed to stretch out the day's feeds and give a good volume of milk throughout the day, you might be able gradually to stop giving this feed. If so, the baby will probably wake a little earlier for the next one. If you are expressing, make sure you do so in good time for your milk to replenish before this feed – you need to do it at least an hour beforehand. Also, make sure you eat well and try to give yourself time to relax.
12am	Breastfeed 30–40 minutes or bottle-feed 4–5 oz (110–140 ml)	If you are expressing, your partner might give this feed. If so, make sure you use the time to get some sleep. Whichever of you is doing the feeding, winding, changing and settling, make sure that everything is laid out ready for the night feeds, and that you have a jug of water next to your bed.
3 or 4am	Breastfeed 30–40 minutes or bottle-feed 4–5 oz (110–140 ml)	As your baby reaches the three-month mark, he may start to take his last feed at around midnight and sleep through till morning. If so, great! But don't expect him to do this consistently until he has started solids, and don't try to force him to do it: keep offering him milk as often as he needs in the night.

As your baby reaches three months, it will become easier to hold him as his neck muscles are stronger and he's bigger all over. You'll know how to manoeuvre around with a lot more ease, and your baby will be happy to be passed around, as he is familiar with your touch, face, smell and voice. All this discrimination allows him to be at ease in a loving environment, but be sure to watch for signs when your baby has had enough of being passed around like the latest issue of *Hello!* magazine.

NAPPY-CHANGING

To avoid nappy rash, change your baby as soon as he soils. Check inside the nappy frequently to make sure it's still dry. The cleaner and drier you keep his bottom, the less likely he is to develop nappy rash. This is especially important if you're bottle-feeding because it increases the possibility of rash. Be aware too when breastfeeding that the odd food you eat may cause nappy rash. Keep that bottom clean!

Whether you use cloth or paper nappies or the new combos, if you've never nappied a baby, you'll find it takes a bit of practice to get it on properly on a squirming, possibly wailing tiny bottom. Don't worry, you'll soon be an old pro. You can easily go through eight to ten nappies a day or more in the beginning. Here's the step by step:

- Make sure you have all supplies within reach before starting.
- Put your baby down on a clean changing mat to avoid vaginal and urine infections.
- Remove the dirty nappy. (If you have a boy, you may get sprayed as his penis is exposed to cold air. To minimise this you can quickly place a clean nappy on him as you remove the old.) Place the dirty nappy out of reach so he won't accidentally fling his leg into poo. This will become more important as he gets older and more mobile.
- Clean the bottom and genitals with a wipe (front to back if you have a girl to avoid vaginal infections). Be sure to get in all the skin folds. When he's newborn, I like using warm water and cotton wool when I'm at home. It's gentler on his delicate skin. Save the disposable wipes for when you're out, and make sure to buy the hypoallergenic ones.

Constant use of wipes can cause nappy rash.
• Pat him dry with his hand towel and make sure to dry in all those folds.
• If a rash appears, I always use Metanium. It's a smelly, yellow, medicated nappy-rash cream. It can stain clothes, but it never stains a baby's bottom and really eliminates the rash quickly. Only use it if you need it. Watch out for other creams as some of them seal in the urine, causing a rash. Also, if he has a rash, make sure you give his bottom air time (time without a nappy on), and don't use any form of soap as it will sting.
• Lift up his bottom, lay down a clean nappy and fasten it so that it's tight enough to keep from leaking but not so tight that it causes marks or discomfort. If you have a boy, make sure his penis is pointing down in the nappy so that he doesn't wet his vest. If the umbilical cord has not yet fallen off, make sure the nappy is below it.
• Put him in a safe spot and clean off the changing mat with disinfectant spray. Put as much of the poo as possible down the toilet to keep the odour down, or use the nappy box to discard.
• If you're using cloth nappies and laundering them yourself, make sure you use a baby-friendly detergent and Napisan to disinfect. Never use fabric softener or antistatic sheets as they can irritate a baby's sensitive skin.

Notice I didn't mention using talcum powder. Research shows it can be dangerous to babies' lungs so stay away. If you must, use corn starch, which absorbs moisture. If you go that route, be sure to wash it off completely each time you change him, especially in the skin folds, as it can breed bacteria. This is your choice, parents; I'm giving you the facts.

A final nappy word: whatever kind

WHEN TO CALL THE DOCTOR OR HEALTH VISITOR

• If the rash is on his thighs, genitals or tummy instead of bottom (a sign of thrush).
• If your baby is six weeks or younger or the rash hasn't gone away within three days.
• If he also has a fever, is eating poorly or losing weight.
• If the rash is spreading to other parts of the body.
• If in addition to redness you see bumps, pimples or open sores.

of nappies you're using, you may find you need to move up in size before the stated weight limit. You'll know it's time when he starts leaking out the back.

PENIS CARE

If your boy has been circumcised, don't clean his penis for four days. Rather, coat a sterile pad with sterile petroleum jelly and place it on the tip after every nappy change to keep it from being irritated by the nappy. After day four, wipe the tip with wet cotton wool and pat dry with a cloth nappy. You may see yellow ooze, a crust or a few drops of blood. If it's oozing blood, call the doctor. If he's not urinating every six hours or so, call the doctor – you'll know by the weight of his nappy. If you notice swelling, there could be an infection, so seek a doctor's advice.

If he's not circumcised, don't retract the foreskin to clean him. This can cause bleeding.

UMBILICAL CORD CARE

Your baby's cord will take two to five weeks to dry up and fall off. Until then, keep it dry and exposed to air as much as possible. Make sure the top of the nappy ends below the belly button. Fold it down if need be. Be sure it's dry after a bath. Never pull it off, even if it's hanging by a thread. If you see oozing pus or redness on the skin around the belly button, consult your doctor or health visitor.

DRESSING

When it comes to dressing your baby, look for clothes that are easy to get on and easy to get off. Take into consideration the textures and fabrics. Some babies have dermatitis or eczema and so should be clothed in cotton to allow the skin to breathe and not get irritated.

There are some babies who don't like being undressed, and there are some babies who won't mind. If yours is one who cries, you're not doing anything wrong. He's just reacting to the change in temperature: he's cold. Place a blanket on top of him as soon as you take his clothes off and that should do the trick.

Your baby's head is the biggest part of his body when he's born, so to dress him in anything that goes over the head, gather up the cloth, stretch it at the neckline with your fingers like you're playing Cat's Cradle and put his head through first and then the arms. It's no different from giving birth! Head first, then shoulders. Gathering up long sleeves, too, will make it much easier to get his arms through. For sleepers, Babygros, undervests and other clothing with poppers, lay it out flat, place him on top of it, then put in his arms and legs, and snap.

Don't mess with shoes – they're actually bad for infant feet. Because babies' bones in their toes are soft, you need to make sure they aren't cramped or they won't grow properly. Don't put them in hard shoes until they're walking – and then only for when they go out. If what he's wearing doesn't cover his feet, put on soft booties or socks to keep those toes warm – and make sure there's plenty of room in there.

Since tiny babies can't regulate their own temperature well, my rule of thumb is to always put on one more layer than you're wearing. But don't overbundle. Being too hot can also be problematic. If you're going to swaddle him, remember to take that into account and dress him more lightly.

NAKED TIME

In order to help the umbilical cord dry and fall off, or to clear up nappy rash, let your newborn lie around naked as much as possible. Make sure he's not cold, especially in the winter.

Half of all newborns develop at least a mild case of jaundice after they come home. It's caused by babies being born with more red blood cells than they need. As the body gets rid of these, it produces a substance called bilirubin. Bilirubin must be absorbed by the liver, and if the liver can't do this quickly enough, the baby develops jaundice, which manifests as yellow cheeks and whites of eyes. Five minutes in the late-afternoon or early-morning sun really helps to prevent this or clear it up – with a hat to protect his eyes, of course.

Be aware that there are two kinds of jaundice, both of which can be dangerous. The more dangerous kind usually develops within 24 hours of being born. If your baby is listless or becomes very yellow, see the doctor to make sure he doesn't have the serious kind. They now have incubators you can

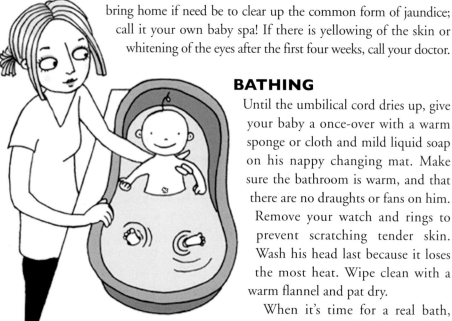

bring home if need be to clear up the common form of jaundice; call it your own baby spa! If there is yellowing of the skin or whitening of the eyes after the first four weeks, call your doctor.

BATHING

Until the umbilical cord dries up, give your baby a once-over with a warm sponge or cloth and mild liquid soap on his nappy changing mat. Make sure the bathroom is warm, and that there are no draughts or fans on him. Remove your watch and rings to prevent scratching tender skin. Wash his head last because it loses the most heat. Wipe clean with a warm flannel and pat dry.

When it's time for a real bath, warm the bathroom and fill the baby bath with a couple of inches of warm water. Test with your elbow. Hold him over the bath, supporting his neck with the thumb and index finger of one hand. With the other hand, wash his head with mild, unscented liquid baby soap. Then place him in the bath, supporting his neck with your forearm, and cradle his body (see illustration). I would recommend bathing him every third day or so, depending on how dry his skin is. The more dry, the less frequent.

Always clean girls' genitals from front to back to avoid infection, and don't use bubble-baths or oils! They

WARM WATER RELIEF

A warm bath in the baby tub can be a good soothing aid for an infant who has a lot of gas or reflux or is irritable. Place one arm under her neck and upper back, the other on her bottom and thighs, and sway her through the water. It's as relaxing for your baby as it is for us adults soaking in a big tub.

NEED TO KNOW

can irritate labias and vaginas. Pat dry, paying particular attention to the creases in the legs and neck.

HEAD CARE

All babies are born with soft spots, or fontanelles, on their skulls, so that the head can grow at the rapid rate it does in the first few months. The one on top of the head at the front closes between 9 and 12 months. The other, on top of the head at the back, is smaller and closes at around three months.

Even though we call them soft spots, the head is really sturdy. Of course you want to be gentle with your baby's head, but despite what you may have been told, you don't have to be too afraid of these spots. You may see them pulsing, and that's normal too.

EAU DE BABY
You know that amazing baby smell you love so much? It actually comes from a release of oil from your baby's head, which, when we smell it, helps us bond. From your baby's fontanelle, 'Baby Chanel'.

If it's seriously indented, it might mean he's dehydrated, so make sure he's feeding enough. Check with the doctor or health visitor if you're concerned.

You may also see thick yellow scales on your baby's head. This is called cradle cap and is a harmless but unsightly skin that peels off. Cradle cap shampoo will help get rid of it, but you can speed the healing along by rubbing natural olive oil into the baby's head, leaving it on for a few hours and then giving his head a gentle circular massage. It will come off.

EAR CARE

Don't mess with the inside of your baby's ears – they're far too sensitive. And never, ever stick a cotton bud in your baby's ear. It can puncture his ear drum and cause permanent hearing problems. Earwax is not harmful in any way, except to your sensibilities. In fact, it actually helps keep out infection. So leave it be unless it's falling out of the outer ear. Then you can remove it. Do, however, clean the lobes and behind the ears.

EYE CARE

Some infants have a yellow crust or discharge in the corner of one or both of their eyes, which is caused by a blocked tear duct. Just wipe with cotton wool that you've wet with warm water. It should clear up in a few days. If it doesn't and the eye starts to swell underneath, and when you lightly press on it with your little finger, it seems spongy, take him to the GP, who will give you a saline solution to clear it up.

As babies get older, sometimes they can get 'sticky eye', or 'red eye', also know as conjunctivitis. You'll know when your child's got it because his eye will be bloodshot, there will be a yellowing crust, and his eyelashes will all stick together. It's highly contagious. See the doctor and be very careful when cleaning his eye to wipe with a warm wet flannel from the tear duct out. Wash your hands and the flannel thoroughly.

BABY ACNE

Newborns often get acne, due to hormone changes from birth. It usually shows up at the one-month mark. Just wash her face every day with water and it will disappear. It's more irritating for parents' vanity than for the baby.

Take note of what your baby's skin is like. Is it hot or cold, smooth or rough? You may find that your baby already has a T-zone, meaning her face is slightly oilier on the forehead, nose and chin. The seasons affect your baby's skin, just as they do ours. As your child gets older, what you may want to do in a harsh winter is smear a very thin, light coat of Vaseline just along her cheekbones.

NAIL-TRIMMING

Babies' fingernails and toenails can scratch their delicate skin and eyes, which can cause an abrasion of the cornea, so it's important to keep nails short.

When a baby is very tiny, up to a month old, you can usually peel his nails with your own fingernails, they're that soft. When you do this, be incredibly careful that you don't go too low, or you'll rip the undersurface as well.

Once the nails harden, then it's time for trimming. Here's how:

• Use baby nail clippers or safety scissors.
• Place him on your knee looking outwards and then hold his hand

and cut his nails as if you're cutting your own. It's much easier.
- Push down gently on the bottom of the nail with your finger. It will make the nail pop up a bit so it's easier to cut.
- Distract him by singing songs and talking about what you're doing. 'Look at this little piggy . . .' That way, he's paying attention to you rather than what you're doing, and before you know it it's done.
- Make sure to cut all the nails straight across so that you don't get ingrown nails.
- You don't have to do all nails on both hands at once. If he's squirming too much, do a few and try again later.
- If you nip the skin, don't panic. Almost every parent has done it once. Just take a gauze pad or tissue and apply pressure until the bleeding stops. It will knit itself back together.

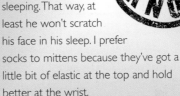

SOCK TRICK

If at first you're too afraid to trim your baby's fingernails, just place a pair of cotton baby socks over his hands while he's sleeping. That way, at least he won't scratch his face in his sleep. I prefer socks to mittens because they've got a little bit of elastic at the top and hold better at the wrist.

Nail-trimming is all about confidence. The more you do it, the more comfortable you and your baby will be. If you're nervous, you'll make your baby nervous. I became an expert nail-trimmer in my nanny years, and mothers used to bring their children round for a visit and a cut!

TAKING A TEMPERATURE

Taking a temperature is an important skill for parents because young babies can run high fevers really fast. The best way to take a newborn's temperature is rectally. A normal rectal temperature is 100.4°F (38°C) in kids under three.

• Make sure you have a rectal thermometer. Use a digital thermometer and mark it with an R. Avoid the glass ones because of possible breakage.
• Turn on the digital thermometer.
• Coat the tip with petroleum jelly.
• Put your baby on his back with his knees up to his tummy on a nappy (in case of accidents).
• Place slowly into your baby's rectum about 1 inch (2.5 cm), and then squeeze his buttocks together. Wait till it beeps.

Call the doctor if his temperature is higher than 100.4°F (38°C) if he's under three months, 101°F (38.3°C) if he's between three and six months, 103°F (39.5°C) if he's six months or older. In the meantime, you can make him more comfortable by stripping him down to a T-shirt. Make sure he gets plenty of fluids – breast or bottle. You can also give him a tepid bath and allow him to air-dry. If that doesn't bring the temperature down, go to hospital.

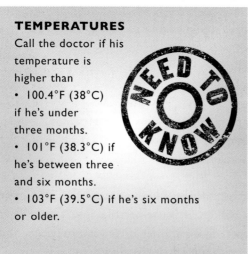

TEMPERATURES
Call the doctor if his temperature is higher than
• 100.4°F (38°C) if he's under three months.
• 101°F (38.3°C) if he's between three and six months.
• 103°F (39.5°C) if he's six months or older.

If you see a temperature that's higher than 104°F (40°C) in the first three months, don't hesitate – take him straight to hospital. It's as simple as that. A high fever can be a serious or dangerous infection.

See the Useful Resources section at the back for a description of common ailments in the first year as well as an emergency first-aid guide.

Febrile seizures or convulsions

Some infants have convulsions when their fever shoots up. They usually aren't dangerous, unless caused by meningitis, but can be incredibly scary for the parent. They can start as early as six months, but they have been known to start before. The baby convulses, eyes rolled back in his head, usually for about two minutes, but it can be up to ten.

If this happens to your baby, place him where he can't hit his head on anything and time the convulsions. Call the ambulance or doctor while timing. Have your baby checked. Something must be causing the fever spike.

MASSAGE

Want to help your baby's digestion, circulation, sleep, growth, lower his stress and yours, and increase bonding between you? Try infant massage. You don't need formal training. Here's all you need to know:

ADMINISTERING MEDICINE

If the doctor prescribes medicine, measure it out carefully and try this method to get it all in:

• Fill the dropper or syringe.
• Take your finger and pull out a corner of her cheek to make a pocket.
• Drip the medicine one drop at a time into the pocket until it's all gone.
• If she hates the taste, try refrigerating it first – cold medicine tastes less strong – or ask the doctor if it comes in any other flavour.
• Slightly tilting her head back will help her swallow when she's a bit older.

NEED TO KNOW

• Do it when your baby is calm, perhaps after feeding, a bath or a nap.
• Heat the room to 75°F (24.8°C) or higher.
• Remove all jewellery and your watch. Make sure your fingernails are short.
• Put down the changing pad and place a soft towel on top of it.
• Remove your baby's clothes and lay him on the towel in his nappy.
• Wash your hands in warm water to heat them up.
• Rub a bit of baby oil, cream or gel between your hands.
• Massage your baby with your fingertips, using a light touch. Do not massage his face with oil.
• **Arms:** rub up and down gently one at a time with a stroking motion.

Legs: squeeze lightly and knead each. **Tummy:** rub one palm in a circle. **Back:** place one hand on each side of his spine and move one up while the other goes down and then reverse. **Chest:** make a heart-shaped motion with your fingertips. **Feet:** use your two thumbs, one thumb on the ball of his foot and one on the heel. Stroke upwards.

• Take no longer than 10–15 minutes.

OUT AND ABOUT

Babies love to be bounced in a pram and I don't see any harm in taking a healthy stroll in the park, meeting a friend for lunch occasionally, or taking him to the supermarket. (You can clip the car seat into the trolley or use one with a built-in seat – after cleaning with a baby wipe.) It's important for you to be able to get some fresh air and meet up with some friends. If you're feeling up to it, then why not? Just don't take him out in a rainstorm. Use your judgement. If you or your baby or friend are sick, then home it is!

Pushchairs should not be used in an upright position until your baby is six months old as the back is not supportive enough until then. However, many now have lie-flat positions that can be used from birth. Car-seat carriers on wheels or prams are best for up to six months.

It's actually easier to take a newborn out than a baby who's mobile. All you need is your changing bag (see Chapter 3), a bottle of formula (unless you're breastfeeding), an infant seat or pram and you're ready to go. If you're lucky, he'll fall asleep during the journey and won't wake up till after you've finished doing what it is you're up to. Just be prepared to leave if he starts crying and won't be comforted.

For longer trips, bring a change of clothes for yourself as well as him in case of emergencies, and always be sure to pack enough formula if bottle-feeding.

BABYPROOFING

In my experience, new parents tend to fall into one of two camps: the 'nothing to worry about' crowd and 'it's all so dangerous it's a miracle any baby survives childhood' group. Both attitudes are problematic because they don't allow you to be realistic while doing as much as you can to prevent accidents. Life comes with hazards, especially for small babies, and it's important to prevent what we can, but we want to do it in a way that doesn't breed hysteria or overwhelming fear in us or our children.

POLLUTANTS

Remember what you learned about your baby's tiny lungs? They absorb twice as many airborne toxins as adults, so keeping him away from pollutants is key to keeping his breathing easy. That means keeping the air around him tobacco-free. Hopefully you don't smoke. If you do, be sure to go outside, and enforce the outside rule for any visitors as well. Infants exposed to second-hand smoke have more colds and ear infections, are more likely to get asthma, pneumonia and bronchitis and are at greater risk of Sudden Infant Death Syndrome (SIDS).

INFANT FIRST AID
Because accidents happen despite our best intentions, I strongly urge you to take an infant first aid and CPR class immediately, if you haven't already, such as the one offered by St John's Ambulance. You can do it individually and privately or in a group, perhaps by getting the parents around the neighbourhood together. I've included basic emergency first aid in Part 4, but this is not meant as a substitute for proper training.

Keep floors and carpets clean – even at this young age, your baby will spend a lot of time on the floor on a blanket or in his Moses basket. This is where heavier chemicals and small particles collect. Keep stairs and hallways free of objects that could trip you when you're carrying him.

BEDROOM

Make sure there is nothing above where your baby sleeps, like a shelf with knick-knacks, which can fall down on to him. Don't leave him alone in your bed and NEVER put him on a waterbed – it's too soft and can cause suffocation. Never cover his mattress with plastic – it's also a smothering hazard.

Never put necklaces, cords attached to dummys or any kind of cord

around his neck. If you use an electrical space heater or night light, make sure it's not near bedding or curtains where it might cause a fire. Be sure to put your baby in fire-retardant sleepwear at bedtime. By law, all sleepsuits are.

Never leave him unattended on the changing table. You never know when he'll learn to roll over. Things happen suddenly. One minute he can't do something and the next minute, boom!

BATHROOM

Never leave a baby alone in the bath, even for a second, even if he's in a bathtub seat. The suction cups can come loose and he might fall face down. Turn the hot water down to the lowest setting and always test the water with your elbow before putting him in to avoid burns. Why the elbow? you may ask. Because our hands are used to being in a lot warmer temperatures and so are less sensitive. Buy a bath thermometer if you like. Store all electrical appliances like hairdryers, curling irons, electrical toothbrushes and so on well away from the bath or sink to prevent electrocution.

KITCHEN

Don't hold your baby while cooking or drinking hot liquids – he might get burned. Place him in the Moses basket a few feet away from you, or place him in his bouncy seat or the baby gym so he's having fun stretching out, grabbing the mirror and the little dangly features above him while you're having coffee. I remember many coffee mornings when the babies were in the middle of the room playing and the mums and nannies were around the edges drinking and chatting.

If you're heating bottles, it's recommended that you put the bottle in a pan of water on the stove rather than use the microwave because microwaves heat unevenly and you can end up scalding him. However, I believe in being realistic and some people will use the microwave because it's very, very quick – 30 seconds and you've got a warm bottle. So use your common sense. Shake it well after heating to avoid hot spots and test the milk on the back of your wrist, then leave it for a bit before you feed your baby.

Keep a list of emergency numbers in the room you're going to be in most often so it's at your fingertips – GP, 999 or 112, the local hospital, the NHS Direct 24-hour helpline (listed in the Useful Addresses section on page 264). Post it on a big corkboard along with other useful info.

CAR

You already know that your baby must be in a rear-facing car seat in the back of the car every time you drive, but think also about what you put next to him in the car. Keep grocery bags and other heavy items in the boot so that if you come to a quick stop or are hit, he won't be injured by flying objects. If you must have them in the car, put them on the floor of the front seat.

Tragic news has been reported of parents who have forgotten about their infant in the back seat of the car on a hot day, which is very dangerous and can lead to death. One way to remember is to put a sticky note on your dashboard every time you take him with you, or put a stuffed animal in the front seat when he's in the back.

To keep the car cool and to protect your baby from the sun while driving, you can get suction-cup window shades. In a pinch, I've rolled down the window a bit, put a towel in and then rolled up the window. Keep the seats cool by putting towels on them too. Park in a shady spot, even if it means walking further, so that the car isn't like a furnace when you get back in.

Protect your baby from the sun totally at this stage, because you shouldn't use sunscreen when he's this tiny. Use carriage shades, umbrellas and a hat with a wide brim and tail that will shade his face and the back of his neck. I call them the Foreign Legion caps. Avoid being outside during the hours of 11 a.m. to 3 p.m. and, if you live somewhere extremely hot, during daylight hours altogether. Damp him down continually with a wet flannel.

PETS

Never leave your baby alone in a room with a pet. Pets can get very jealous and do unpredictable things, even the most gentle ones. When your baby is very young, avoid letting the pet go near your baby at all. In fact, distance is best for the first year. To your pet, this tiny creature is a stranger – one that makes a lot of noise and smells funny. As your baby gets older, he may unintentionally provoke the pet by pulling its tail or grabbing its fur. Be aware also that pets can cause allergies. I know this first hand! Separation is especially important if your baby has asthma or was born with eczema, and also helps prevent pets from passing on ticks, ringworm and other unpleasantnesses.

If you are thinking of getting a pet, wait until your child is older. If you already have one, and if you think it will be a burden to manage the animal as well as your newborn, consider boarding it for the first week or two or having a friend take it. If you don't think it's going to be a burden, I'm assuming that's because you and your partner have sat down to work out who's going to take care of the animal, and that together you're going to be responsible for not leaving your baby in a room where the animal is. Consider a baby gate to keep them separated. And never tie a dog's lead to the pram while walking – the dog can tip it over!

SHAKEN BABY SYNDROME

No matter how frustrated, annoyed, impatient or angry you get, *never shake your baby*. It can permanently damage his brain and spinal cord, causing blindness, paralysis and death. As I have said before, if he won't stop crying and it's getting on your last nerve, put him down in his basket and take a breather in another room. Call a friend or relative for help, or a parent helpline (see Useful Addresses on page 263).

I've put this warning in a couple of places because parents feel a strong need to control their baby's crying. The feeling of helplessness that arises when you can't leads to frustration that can then lead to anger. It's important to understand this, because the more you understand that you can't control your baby's crying, and that what you need at certain times is patience, the less frustrated you'll feel.

STIMULATION AND EXPLORATIONS

LEARNING THROUGH PLAY

You know about the importance of taking care of your baby's physical needs. Now it's time to focus on his mental and emotional ones. Stimulating your baby's brain is key to intellectual development and mental health. His brain is very active – twice as active as an adult's. Researchers estimate that 50 per cent of the human's brain development occurs in the first six months of life and 70 per cent is complete by the end of the first year. That's an awfully large proportion, and it shows why it's especially important to interact with your baby throughout the first year.

This is not all about giving him fancy educational toys. Research is now revealing that babies' brains actually get formed by interaction with people and explorations in their environment. It's like an electrical circuit, all potentiality, waiting for you to switch the current on through interaction and stimulation. So the best things you can do are cuddling and interacting with him as much as possible when he's awake, and encouraging him to reach the healthy developmental milestones that you learned about in the Developmental Overview.

These are some of the crucial abilities you'll be helping to stimulate:

- auditory development, hearing and speaking
- visual development, seeing at close and far range, as well as visual tracking, the ability to follow something with the eyes, visual memory, the ability to recall faces, images and objects, all of which are crucial in learning to read
- balance, the ability to maintain body positions against the force of gravity
- eye–foot coordination, gauging distance and depth with the eyes and processing that information to coordinate movement
- eye–hand coordination, directing the position and the motion of the hands in response to visual information to grasp things
- fine motor skills, which allow hand motions like picking up small objects and handling things like spoons

- gross motor skills, which enable movement of the whole body in a coordinated way
- object permanence, the concept that an object or a person exists even if you can't see them
- trust, knowing that one's basic needs will be cared for.

Remember, as I said in the Developmental Overview, babies progress at different paces and some achieve skills quicker than others. It's important to notice when he's achieved a milestone so that you can encourage him to move on to the next thing and not wait just because he's not a certain age. For example, as soon as you see your baby gaining more control over his arms, hands and wrists, then it's time to encourage more fine motor development.

On page 135, I give a list of all the sorts of toys your baby can enjoy over the year rather than putting them in the age stages – it's helpful to know all the options and choose what works for your baby at any given point. In general, toys for newborns are made of soft fabric so they are easier to grasp. As babies get older, toys are more likely to be made of wood or plastic. When purchasing, do take note of the recommended age on the packaging to get an idea of appropriateness. However, be aware that it may not be right for your child.

Even with the best intentions, you will end up with things that he won't be able to use yet. For instance, someone might buy him a little wooden tricycle, which you know he can't ride. Although you can put him on top of it and then hold him and push it, things that are just too old need to be put aside until he can really enjoy them. There's nothing worse than using something way beyond his level of development; it will cause frustration for your baby and you.

Likewise, don't hang on to toys that he's developed beyond. I've gone into many homes recently where toddlers are still playing with baby toys. You want to stay one step ahead and add things that will challenge him. Bag up the newborn toys once he's passed that stage and save them for the next baby, or give them to charity or a friend or relative.

Don't plop him in front of the telly. TV and DVDs don't provide the kind of interaction a baby needs and can cause obesity later due to lack of movement. If you're desperate for a break, a few minutes won't hurt, but it shouldn't be a regular thing.

The signs of isolation speak volumes when a child has not been given human interaction. The more you put in in the early years, the greater the pay-off down the line. When I walk into a house, I can see where there's been no stimulation because the child is not where he would be if he'd been given the time and interaction. It affects his physical and emotional development, and intellect. Stimulation takes time. Fortunately, most parents find it a lot of fun too.

When playing, watch for signs of tiredness – turning away, getting irritable. A baby doesn't have a long attention span and will soon make it obvious that he's had enough. Read your baby's cues. Sometimes it's just not the right time – perhaps when he's just been fed and has wind. This is a process of trial and error. You may find, when you try something, that your baby doesn't respond. Try something else.

Be realistic as well. You're not an amusement park. You don't have to fill every minute of the day, or give your child one long roller-coaster ride. You've got other things to take care of. You want to give short spurts of stimulation, which will allow you to feel content as a parent and your baby to feel content with the time she's spent with you.

Also, a big part of healthy stimulation is creating experiences for others within your trusted circle to connect with your baby. The task shouldn't all fall on you.

A PLAYFUL ATTITUDE

It's important not to make this a chore. As much as we want our babies to reach those milestones, it's not about ticking them off: 'Okay, right, yesterday I worked on his visual stimulation, so today I'll work on his audio.' It should feel unforced. Play comes naturally to babies, so it's crucial that you feel the same way, even if it's a bit awkward at the beginning. Some parents have never been around babies, and all of a sudden there he is and you think, 'Right, what do I do?' Have fun!

Babies aren't born knowing the world is a wonderful place. You are their teacher. You are showing them how beautiful the world is, how much fun it is, building that knowledge in everything you do with them. It's actually very inspiring – you are creating your baby's world for him. You can see why it's so important that you play together.

I was told recently by one father that too much information makes parents feel overloaded and afraid. In this book I'm trying to go back to basics, so in this section you'll find very simple things you can do with little or no equipment. What follows are suggestions to get you started.

PLAY IDEAS

When your baby is first born, the most important thing is to have lots of face-to-face time. Lots of hugs, lots of kisses, talking in that lovely high-pitched, warm voice, calling his name. Eventually he'll respond with a head turn, a gurgle, a smile. Being in front of a tiny baby brings out the mush in most of us, but if it doesn't, don't worry about it. Just start off doing something.

Everything is new for your baby. Don't be surprised if you become overly enthusiastic and give your baby such a very large and noisy kiss or jiggle that he cries. Some newborns take sudden noises or movements with a pinch of salt and won't move at all, while others will be quite frightened. You're learning as fast as your baby right now. I like to play around with my voice and make different noises as well as sing different lullabies to find his preferences.

Equally important is just to allow your baby to be. He's going to be sleeping an awful lot, particularly for the first four weeks, so it's important to find a balance between stimulating your baby and having still time with him on your lap, gazing into his eyes and talking softly. The sound of your voice and the feel of your hands are very reassuring.

A lot of this year is about preparing for future development. In the beginning, babies can only see in black and white, but we still give them coloured objects. We know they're not going to read at one year old, but we still read them stories. They don't get it, but doing it now helps them get it later.

Sensory stimulation

Stimulate their sense of touch, sound, and sight. Gently shake a variety of little rattles so he hears different things. Place him on his mat and scrunch up pieces of paper for new sounds. Take a make-up brush or feather and stroke his arms, legs and face. How does he respond?

Even though babies are fascinated by sounds and voices because they heard them in the womb, they're not able to locate where the sound has come from, so another thing you can do is to rattle or make a noisy toy move from left to right in front of your baby so that he can start to establish where the noise is coming from. Once he recognises sounds in front of him, make the sound on the side and see if he turns his head.

As a newborn, his vision is blurry, but that doesn't mean that you can't give him objects within a close range to look at. Put objects by the bouncer seat as well as a mobile overhead. You'll know when he's starting to focus because he'll aim towards something with a hand. That's when you can start putting objects above him so he learns he can lift his eyes and move his head to see. You're helping him develop his vision-tracking. This is also when it's good to hang a pretty thing he can see from his rear-facing car seat.

Talk it up

Stimulate your child with lots of talk. Baby-talk is fine, but intersperse it with adult words too so you challenge her language development. Babies who are spoken to are more assertive and learn language faster. I always tell parents to be animated, because babies absolutely love it.

For some parents, it's really difficult to start talking. There you are staring at your baby, thinking, 'What am I going to say?' Just say what you see: 'You've got lovely big eyes. Oh, and what a teeny little chin.' You can say almost anything, as long as it's not a rant about your terrible day.

Another easy way to start is to pick up your baby and show her herself in a mirror: 'Who's this, who's this?' For now she won't know, but the time will come when she coos and smiles and really shows interest in what you're saying. Remember, the more opportunities you give her to practise these skills, the sooner they develop.

Let your inner pop star out!

One key skill as a parent is to learn to be comfortable singing. Let your inner pop star out! Children love music. In the beginning, sing lullabies. Don't know any? Why should you? Go out and buy the CD and get the nursery rhyme book while you're at it. Or be your own Elton John and make up lyrics.

Humming is fabulous too because it creates a soothing vibration, for you and your baby. Hum or sing when bathing, feeding, dressing, driving, and so on and you'll find those tasks are easier on both of you.

Tummy time

Since she must sleep on her back for safety, as she approaches the two-month mark or so, be sure to give her 'tummy time' when she's awake to help physical development – babies can raise their heads when they're on their stomachs more easily at first than when they're on their backs. But her neck muscles must be strong enough before you do this or she'll just end up face down on the mat.

Partly why I'm against holding babies all day is that it's good for them to be lying down on the floor with you beside them, on their backs at first, tickling and touching them, so they see you and interact with you while having their own space. Get down on the floor and put props in front of your child's face to stimulate his visual ability. Hold objects about 8–15 inches (20–40 cm) away so he can see them well. Help your baby gain eye–hand coordination by moving objects in front of or above him that he can bat at.

'Play it again, Sam'

Repetition is incredibly important. Sing the same songs, recite the same nursery rhymes and rattle the same rattle over and over. These repetitions will eventually make him smile, turn round and gurgle. He's recognising the pattern, which causes great delight. He will remember and eventually copy what he's been taught.

Change of scenery

Take your baby with you from room to room and out and about. He'll love the stimulation of new sights, sounds and smells. Introduce him to other children and adults, one at a time if you have a shy, sensitive child. Believe it or not, even babies this young get bored!

TOYS FOR THE FIRST YEAR

Musical games and toys	birth onwards
Bubbles	birth onwards
Coloured scarves	birth onwards
Mirrors	birth onwards
Finger puppets	birth onwards
Cuddly toys	birth onwards
Soft balls	birth onwards
Press-and-turn toys, push-down spinning tops	three months onwards
Books, especially cloth and board	three months onwards
Bath toys	six months onwards
Boxes	six months onwards
Tupperware or plastic bowls and big wooden spoon	six months onwards
Tunnels	six months onwards
Buckets	six months onwards
Dolls	nine months onwards
Plastic telephones with flashing lights	nine months onwards
Plastic keys/cell phones	nine months onwards
Shape/numbers/animal sorters	nine months onwards
Stacking rings/stacking cups/blocks	nine months onwards
Large wooden-knob floor puzzles	nine months onwards
Pull-and-push toys like dogs and caterpillars on leads, activity walkers	nine months onwards
Inflatable balls to lean on	nine months onwards
Wendy house/tent	a year onwards
Role-play equipment: pots and pans, dustpan and brush	a year onwards
Activity train sets	a year onwards
Rides/wooden bike	a year onwards
Finger paints and finger crayons for drawing	a year onwards (if very advanced)
YOU	ALWAYS!

CLASSES

Baby activity classes are lovely because they offer a wider sort of human interaction. Parents ask me when's a good time to start and I say it's entirely up to you. If you're wondering what a good age is for a particular activity, most classes will tell you the starting age. In addition to paid classes, churches have playgroups and coffee mornings, and there are also organised activities at workplaces. Check around.

Chapter 5
Three to Six Months

PARENTS' JOURNEY

Well done! You've come a long way in a short time. Things are getting easier, aren't they? Good on you! You've paid attention to your baby and are starting to be able to see patterns in what various cries mean, and when she eats and sleeps. You can read her better and so have more calm moments. You've just spent three months together and know her likes and dislikes, her favourite rattle, her preferred winding position. You're becoming more in sync, in tune, which allows you to be one step ahead of your baby. Rather than just respond to her needs, you start to anticipate them. You're halfway between the parent who *wants* to know everything and the one who *does* know everything about your baby!

By now, her temperament is showing itself. I've seen lots of parents make jokes about that: 'Oh yeah, she likes her food, just like your side of the family!' You're getting your sense of humour back again, aren't you? In the very beginning, everything is serious as you want to get it right. Now you've earned your badge so you can begin to have a bit more fun. Plus she's getting more active, so the process of baby care may be more enjoyable for you. With all the smiles and the laughs, you get feedback that you're on the right track.

'You're halfway between the parent who *wants* to know everything and the one who *does* know everything about your baby!'

As much as you're recognising what your baby needs, you and your spouse are recognising what you need as well. You know when you need some time for yourself and how to balance baby care with the rest of your life. Hopefully you're not as tired. You've got some kind of acceptable house management going on and your emotions aren't so much on the surface. You remember feeling exhausted or overwhelmed, but the feelings themselves are (hopefully) gone. Your feet have definitely touched the ground.

You've also learned from your mistakes: 'I went to the park and didn't bring any wipes with me.' Those mistakes have taught you to be adaptable – you know you can figure out what to do even when you don't have the proper equipment. Your competence and confidence are growing. Because you did it from 0–3 months, you know that you can do it from 3–6 months, right?

WHAT YOU MIGHT NOTICE As this period progresses, you might find your baby doing the following:
• Laughing
• Putting up his arms to be held
• Rolling over
• Learning to sit up

This stage is about creating lots of opportunities to stimulate your baby's development. This is the time to get out into the world more together – to join 'Mummy and me'-type classes, which are as much for you to bond with other mums as for your baby's sake. You may find yourselves starting to seek out more resources and more connection to other parents going through the same stage. It helps to recognise that you're not alone: 'Oh, hey! Our baby has the same cold that Johnny down the road has.' And, 'I'm not the only one who's not up for sex every night.'

You've entered a world where the more you know, the more you want to seek and find even more resources. You want more information because you recognise that you have more choices now, and that's very empowering. You want to be the best. You wanted to be the best in the beginning, but now you're secure enough to feel quite comfortable that you don't know it all. Embrace your exploration, because it will lead you to become even more confident.

One of the greatest things about having a baby is that you continue to love every day. Your love just grows and grows. That's because you've spent more and more time together. And it's only the beginning of that wonderful connection.

DEVELOPMENTAL OVERVIEW

PHYSICAL DEVELOPMENT

He'll continue to gain 1.5–2 lb (680–900 g) a month on average at this stage, but how much he weighs and how long he is are less important than the fact that he is growing. Every baby has his own growth rate, which your doctor will track. As long as he's consistently growing at the same rate, there's no need for alarm. Talk to the doctor if you have concerns.

He'll be awake more during the day now, and since his stomach is larger, he will probably not need the middle-of-the-night feeding. As a result, by four months, he – and you – will be sleeping seven to eight hours at a go. How lovely! If this isn't happening, he may need more stimulation in the evening or more food, so feed for longer or give him an extra feed just before going down for the night.

This time is all about beginning to move, which he will learn in stages as his head and neck muscles and sense of balance develop. First, he'll hold up his head and shoulders when placed on his tummy. Then, at around five months, he'll do a baby push-up. You'll see him 'swimming' on his tummy too, kicking his legs and waving his arms with head up. It will be easy to pull him into a standing position.

At some point he'll roll over, usually from front to back first. This often happens 'out of the blue', which is why you should never leave a baby unattended on any high surface. In the beginning, once he's rolled on to his back he's stranded because his muscles aren't strong enough to flip him back on to his tummy. By six months, however, he'll be doing it like a pro and will begin to pull himself across the floor on his tummy, the first step towards crawling. At the six-month mark, he'll also be able to sit up unassisted and to stand when you hold him up.

By month four, his little hands will put things in his mouth, so beware what you leave within his grasp. He'll grab his toes and they might go into his mouth too. He doesn't know how to use his thumb, though – that doesn't kick in until about nine months – so he'll be clumsy. Larger objects are easier to grasp than small ones, and you may find he grips tightly on to things, including your hair or clothes.

He'll start to explore other parts of his body too, such as his genitals, while being changed. Put something just out of reach and he'll struggle to get to it. He'll begin splashing in the bath and put everything in his mouth.

By this time, he'll be imitating sounds you make and be able to hear softer sounds. His vision continues to develop, and he'll probably prefer objects that are blue or red. He can actually tell the difference now between a real face and a photo of a face.

At around six months, he'll probably get his first tooth, but there is tremendous variation with this. Some babies are born with a tooth; others don't have even one by their first birthday.

SOCIAL AND EMOTIONAL DEVELOPMENT

Besides smiles and sounds, at four months your baby will start to respond to you by raising his arms up to be picked up. That's such a precious moment.

So is his first laugh, which typically occurs in the fifth month. You'll find yourself doing all kinds of things to hear that wonderful giggle. Around this time, he'll discover cause and effect – 'The rattle makes a noise when I shake it. And Mummy and Daddy also react when I drop something on the ground.' He'll begin to drop things on purpose to get a response from you. He's experiencing his environment and learning object constancy. You may also see signs that he has a memory of people and routines, and he may become attached to a particular toy. He'll look forward to feeding as a social time, not just nourishment.

At five months, she may exhibit signs of jealousy if you hold other babies and will begin to be wary of strangers, although she may not yet have full-blown stranger anxiety. This is when she also starts to demonstrate her preferences – turning her head if she's not hungry and expressing frustration at not being able to do something she wants. You'll begin to hear sounds that indicate emotions – fear, anger, dislike. That angry cry sounds different from the tired or hungry one.

By month six, he will begin to imitate your emotions and actions. Try it – smile and see what he does. Now frown.

WHEN TO CALL THE HEALTH VISITOR OR DOCTOR

Refuses to cuddle by four months

•

Shows no affection for the primary caretaker

•

Can't sit with help by six or seven months

•

Doesn't respond to sounds

•

Doesn't laugh by six months

Bang a toy. Sneeze. You'll be amazed at what a mimic he is. He'll start imitating sounds in combinations (da, da, da) and watch your mouth closely when you speak. You may see him respond to music too, by bouncing, humming or swaying.

Is he easy-going or headstrong? Calm or boisterous? Shy or outgoing? These inborn tendencies will emerge even more strongly now. There's not a lot you can do to change your baby's temperament. It's up to you to adapt – with more routine and calm for the highly strung child, more quiet attention and time to warm up to a new situation for the shy one, more physical stimulation for the boisterous one. It's your job to pay attention to who this little one is and what he needs, and then provide that to the best of your ability.

SETTING FIRM GROUND

ROUTINES

You have a history to fall back on now. You can look back and see the good that's been happening, and think, 'Oh, that works! That's what I'm going to do now because that worked yesterday.' As you create more of a routine, understand that babies are sometimes unpredictable. Things may work on Wednesday and not on Friday. You've got to have a certain amount of patience – you can't just try something once and give up if it doesn't work. And remember, all kinds of things can disrupt your routine. It's your job to flex around those and then re-establish. It's about creating cornerstones to your routine so it doesn't matter if the sides fall in occasionally.

FEEDING

Current guidelines state that you should not feed your baby anything but milk (either breast or formula) until they are six months old. If you decide to wean at any time before six months, this constitutes early weaning, and you must ask your doctor or health visitor for advice on how to proceed and what foods are safe. You must never introduce solid foods before your baby is four months old. As your baby grows, it will take less time to feed him as you and he get the hang of it. However, the older he gets, the more he will look around and be curious. Try to keep him focused by creating a calm, quiet feeding environment, otherwise you'll find he's not feeding enough, only to get hungry an hour later.

At six months, it's time to add solid foods to your baby's diet. If you are tempted to start weaning before this (early weaning), make sure that you consult medical advice before going ahead.

The good news about adding solid foods is that he'll be more likely to sleep through the night because his tummy will be fuller. At the beginning, though, the majority of his nourishment will still come from milk or formula.

Food should be introduced gradually, a few spoonfuls at a particular mealtime. Only give one type of food at a time so you can judge whether something creates a bad reaction or he doesn't like it. Start with baby cereal (rice cereal is great because it rarely causes allergies) mixed with formula, breast milk or cooled boiled water. Put a tiny bit on a baby spoon or your finger to begin with.

Expect a look of unsureness when he first tastes solids. The flavour and texture are very different from milk. If he spits it out, it doesn't necessarily mean he doesn't like it – it might be that he's trying to figure out what to do. If he refuses altogether, wait a week or try another food. A couple of spoonfuls to start with is just fine. When he turns his head away, that's a sign he's full or doesn't like it. Don't force it. Also, be aware that babies of four to six months poke their tongues in and out to make saliva to water down the food before swallowing it, so don't interpret that as a rejection.

At first, feeding will be very messy. Make sure you use a big bib and have my fave, a clean mussy on your shoulder. Put a plastic mat or towel under the high chair or infant seat if you're really worried about mess. Use a plastic spoon. He may roll the food around a lot, exploring the experience of eating, and lots may land on the floor or bib or food tray. Eventually he'll get the hang of it. You want to work up to a dozen spoonfuls or so at a meal.

CORNERSTONE ROUTINE 3–6 MONTHS

The baby should have learned to feed more quickly at this point, which gives you more time to enjoy his company in between meals and naps. He will also be using more energy as he learns to do more and more, so make sure you are allowing for this by giving him enough to eat at each meal. Paediatricians recommend that you introduce solids to your baby's diet at six months, the very end of this period.

Time all feeds from when your baby begins to feed.

7am	Breastfeed 20–40 minutes or bottle-feed 5–6 oz (140–170 ml)	After the baby has fed, winded, changed and had a bit of stimulation, put him down for a nap. Don't forget to feed yourself while he's napping! By six months, this naptime may have reduced from two hours to about an hour, giving you some fun playtime together.
10am	Breastfeed 20–40 minutes or bottle-feed 5–6 oz (140–170 ml)	At six months (but not before unless you have been advised to by your doctor or health visitor) you might offer a couple of spoonfuls of baby rice or fruit puree during this feed. Make sure you only do this halfway through the milk feed: milk is still the baby's most important source of nutrition and it is important you don't reduce the amount your baby is getting. After this feed he should have lots of energy for some good stimulation time with you, either one-on-one or at a baby group, but it's important he also gets a really good sleep before lunchtime.
2pm	Breastfeed 20–40 minutes or bottle-feed 5–6 oz (140–170 ml)	At three months, your baby will still need an afternoon catnap of about 30 minutes between now and teatime, but you might find that it's possible to cut this out as you reach the six-month mark, especially if the baby is finding it difficult to settle for the night after supper.

Time	Feed	Notes
6pm	Breastfeed 20–40 minutes or bottle-feed 5–6 oz (140-170 ml)	After feeding and winding, put the baby into his night-time clothes and settle him down for the night. Somewhere around four to six months, you might decide to put the baby to sleep in his own room rather than next to you at night. You might give them a musical mobile to listen to or a favourite stuffed animal to hold to help them drift off to sleep.
11pm	Breastfeed 20–40 minutes or bottle-feed 5–6 oz (140–170 ml)	Your partner might give this feed from a bottle, using either expressed milk or possibly formula, which some people believe is heavier in the tummy and helps them sleep longer.
3 or 4am	Breastfeed 20–40 minutes or bottle-feed 5–6 oz (140–170 ml)	Until your baby is firmly established on solids you will have to keep feeding him if he asks for it in the night. Be patient: there's not long to go until you can try to get him to sleep through.

SLEEPING THROUGH THE NIGHT

According to the National Sleep Foundation, at between three and eleven months your baby should be sleeping 9–12 hours a night plus having one to four naps a day of 30 minutes to 2 hours for a total of 12–15 hours. I wholeheartedly agree.

At five or six months your baby may start sleeping through (but remember you cannot expect this to happen consistently until your baby is firmly established on solids) so you can create a proper bedtime routine of about 20 minutes: perhaps a massage, rocking, then a lullaby and off to bed. The idea is to get him drowsy, not asleep, so he can learn to go to sleep on his own. In the 6–9 months section, you'll learn the Controlled-crying Technique to get him to sleep through the night, but I would not try this before six months.

Between four and six months, you have the choice of putting your baby in his own room if you have the option. Start by placing the Moses basket into the cot so that he'll feel secure – putting him in straight away can make him feel rather insecure with so much space around him. Then, after a couple days, place your baby down for his naps directly in the cot and then, when he's fine with that, in the evening. You can also buy a baby-sleeping bolster (they look like angel wings!) – you place the baby in the middle and there's a tiny rolled pad either side that makes him feel more secure. Ensure there is no suffocation hazard.

Put that little baby mobile up or the little teddy with a string that pulls down and makes a sweet lullaby. The ritual will become very pleasant as he begins to understand that when he goes into the cot and the music is played, it's time for sleep. You're going to have a lot more alert and astute a baby at six months, so it is important to make sure that any mobile that's hanging over the cot is not so low that your baby could do any harm to himself with ribbons or cords if he grabbed hold of it and pulled it down.

I'm not against babies holding on to a mussy, favourite blankie or stuffed animal that smells of themselves for years and years to go to sleep. I even know some parents who've still got their blankies as a keepsake.

Sometimes babies get muddled and think day is night and night is day. To get him back on a normal schedule, make sure it's really bright in the morning and dark in the evening. Keep him as active and stimulated in the day, and as quiet and placid in the evening as possible. He'll get with the programme.

CRYING

By now you're probably much better at figuring out why your baby is crying. One more reason for crying to consider now is his need for stimulation. Babies often cry from boredom.

When you have something to do, put him in a bouncy seat where he can sit properly and watch you, which allows him to be stimulated visually and aurally without having to be held. If he continues to cry, do what you're going to do and then go up to him and offer reassurance with hugs and kisses. Pick him up, give him cuddles and then put him back down again. Then go back to what you were doing and say, 'Mummy's here, look, Mummy's here. Look what I'm doing.' Eventually his crying will become sporadic and then he will stop to take note, watch and listen.

PRAISE

Whenever your baby does something right, let him know. Praise him for feeding, for taking a good nap, for playing, for sitting in the car seat. Verbal praise creates encouragement and helps development. Your little one is never too young for praise!

KEEPING WARM TO STAY ASLEEP

As your baby gets older you may want to move away from the swaddling and use a baby sleep bag. I swear by them. Babies often wake up because they've become too cold as their temperature drops when they're sleeping. Sleep bags not only keep them warm, but help prevent overheating as they come in a variety of breathable fabrics. You can get summer ones that are lighter in tog value and quilted ones for the winter.

PARENTCRAFT

NAPPY-CHANGING

As your baby gets more active, be sure to give her something to play with while you're changing her. There will be less squirming, and the process will go faster.

DRESSING

So many parents struggle to get their kids dressed at this age because they're wriggling around and it becomes a whole trauma just trying to put on a pair of trousers. I think the best thing to do is just to work with the baby. Give him something to distract himself with, and just do it as quickly as possible.

I believe in using baby tights from the age of three months. Yes, boys and all. Shakespeare did it. Remember, it's all about layering to keep them warm.

SKINCARE

As you start introducing solids, if you see an outbreak of 'acne', it's probably not. It's most likely an allergic reaction to something she's eaten. Be aware very, very quickly and try to figure out what she's reacting to.

BATHING

I think it's fine for parents to get into the bathtub with their little ones from the three-month mark. There's something quite beautiful about spending time together in the water. You feel confident, and your baby's confident in the water with you. It's a wonderful transition from the small plastic tub to putting them into the big bath by themselves when they can sit up.

BABYPROOFING YOU

You've created a safe environment for your baby through babyproofing, but what about protecting yourself from your baby? I'm talking about hair- and earring-grabbing and other death-grip activities your little one will now be able to engage in. You can minimise painful situations by wearing hair back if it's long and not wearing earrings or necklaces, particularly dangly ones, around your baby. Ditto for ties, Dad. Make sure you take them off before holding him.

I spent years carrying scrunchies on my wrist like bangles so that I could wear my hair down and then pull it up when necessary. Sometimes I like to wear it down to tickle babies with it. After 17 years, it's become a habit. Even while filming, I'm always being told to leave my hairbands off my wrists. There used to be a little cartoon called Bod on the telly with a character named Aunt Flo. I always joke that I look like Flo with a bun on the top of my head – the only place I can guarantee my hair won't be grabbed.

And if you're one of those mums or dads with lots of piercings, watch out for those as well. Make sure they're studs and not dangling all over the place, otherwise you just may get caught.

MOUTH CARE

Once you start feeding solids, you should start mouth-cleaning, even if there are no teeth. Those gums are getting covered in gunk! You can use a dampened soft infant toothbrush, a piece of wet gauze or a fingertip brush.

No toothpaste, though. They all contain fluoride, and swallowing fluoride can harm the enamel of forming teeth.

And remember, no putting your baby to sleep with a bottle in his mouth. It leads to tooth decay, tooth pain and early loss of milk teeth. Too much milk can alter the development process so that molars appear later: it's too much milk for the milk teeth.

OUT AND ABOUT

Despite the logistical challenges, taking an infant on a trip is actually easier to do before they're crawling or walking, so consider taking that trip, via plane or car, now. And be sure that your destination is babyproofed.

No matter what their age, travelling with children is all about preparation – making sure that you know exactly how long you're going for and what the weather is like where you're going so that you have the right clothing, sunblock, shades for the pushchair, umbrellas, mosquito net or whatever they'll need for protection. Bring extra outfits, not only for your baby but for you in case of messes, and be sure you get everything in place three days before so you avoid last-minute rushing around.

In 17 years of nannying, I have very successfully gone on holiday with many families and it's been an absolute delight, even when the journey has been as long as nine or ten hours on a plane with an infant. In addition to good preparation, the key is sticking as much as possible to the baby's routine.

Plane travel

Once your baby gets past the first few months and his immune system is a bit more developed, you can consider plane trips. It's a 50/50 chance whether the flights will go well or badly. Anyone who's sat next to a screaming baby on a long flight knows what I'm talking about. To increase the chances of a good experience:

- Go at the time your baby is most likely to sleep.
- Call the airline to find out whether they provide bassinets. Know, however, that if the flight is bumpy, they will ask you to hold your baby in your arms. The safest thing to do is to purchase his own seat and strap him in using his car seat.
- Also find out from the airline exactly what you can carry on. Due to security restrictions, this changes often.
- Check your pushchair and car seat in at the plane door, unless you've bought a seat for your child, in which case take the seat on with you.
- Bring lots of powdered formula if you're bottle-feeding and ask the flight attendants for water to mix it with. You may have the liquid kind or pre-made bottles confiscated at the gate due to liquid restrictions.
- If he's on solids, don't forget to pack those as well.
- Board before everyone else if possible so you have time and space to settle. Ask the stewards.
- Feed your baby during take-off and landing to avoid ear pain due to changes in air pressure.
- Drink extra fluids, especially if you're nursing, to avoid dehydration.
- Put down the nappy pad from your changing bag and change your baby on your seat rather than in the cramped, potentially overused bathroom.

• Don't forget to take rattles, favourite toys and baby books, mussy and blankie. A few things to do will go a long way towards preserving the sanity of everyone on the plane.

Plane travel with babies doesn't have to be a big dramatic experience. You can make it easier with preparation and positivity. You're either going to embrace it and have a good experience or you're not. The choice is yours, so make it a happy one. At the end of the day, if your baby is crying a lot, remember he's not doing it to annoy everybody on the plane. It's about time people showed more consideration in this situation. Babies cry. Let's hope the rest of society can learn to embrace this and be a little bit more compassionate.

Car trips

Many families find car trips easier with infants because you have the flexibility of being able to stop anywhere and take a breather. The motion of the car normally gets babies sleeping really well, too. Car trips are also good because you don't have the added pressure of everybody looking at you if your baby is crying – it's just you and your family in the car, which allows you to feel a little bit more relaxed.

The list of what to bring is the same as for the plane.

BABYPROOFING

Before your baby gets mobile, it's time to make sure you've got all hazards out of reach – pesticides, detergents, alcohol, bleach, plant fertiliser, house plants (many are poisonous if eaten), medicines – anything he can put into his mouth that might harm him should be stored up high or in locked cupboards. The same goes for sharp objects – knives, scissors, and so on.

There are plenty of safety gadgets you can buy. Make sure you take the time to do this! These things can be complicated, but half an hour spent fixing a lock on that door could very well save your child's life because one minute he isn't even able to crawl and the next, he's in the cupboard pulling everything out and putting things in his mouth.

Make sure you check every room. I've seen families put a lock on the kitchen cleaning supplies and forget they keep their bathroom cleaning stuff in cupboards that can easily be pulled open.

Store all medicines and liquids in their original containers so you can tell what they are and what to do in case of ingestion. Throw old medicines away into a container that can't be opened.

Now is also the time to cover all plug sockets so he can't stick his tiny finger in there and to put window guards on all dangerous windows. Put bulbs in any empty light fittings. Get a lead tidy to cover up the wires for your TV, DVD player, and so on.

Make sure humidifiers, portable heaters and the like are beyond his reach when he's in his cot.

Bags can suffocate. Get rid of plastic dry-cleaning and shopping bags immediately. If you save them to use again, get a shopping-bag tidy and hang it up high, somewhere out of reach.

SCAN DAILY

By six months, anything within reach will get scooped up and popped in his mouth, so be sure that all toys he can get hold of have no small parts that can break off (like his older brother's car wheels, for instance). Keep older children's toys away from the baby's. Ditto pet toys and pet food.

Whenever you put him down, scout around to make sure there are no small items around that he could choke on. Also make sure there's nothing between the sofa cushions. When there's a baby around, I become like a metal detector, Bip-Bip-Bip-Bip! I find all kinds of things. For instance, Dad's in a rush in the morning and he's had his shirt dry-cleaned and it has pins in it. And I find a pin on the floor! Be sure to scan, scan, scan every day.

COMMON CHOKING HAZARDS

- coins
- buttons
- beads
- marbles
- rings
- earrings
- pins
- pen and marker caps
- drawing pins
- paper clips
- balloons
- foam balls that compress
- toy car wheels
- plastic eyeballs from teddies and dolls
- button-sized batteries
- bottle caps

Small round items are extreme choking hazards because babies' airways are small and their muscles aren't well developed, so they have more trouble swallowing than adults. That's why, when you begin to serve solid food at around four months, it should be puréed. And never leave him alone when eating (more on this later).

If you're in doubt whether or not something is a choking hazard, you can buy a choke tube or small-parts tester, or use a toilet paper roll tube. If it can fit inside, it's too small.

Make sure the high chair is not near a window or any appliances, and make sure you keep all hot liquids – coffee, tea, soup – out of reach. Absolutely, positively clip your child into the high chair! My word, the number of parents who do not put the harness over him because he cries at being clipped in. Here's one of your first chances as a parent to do what's right, regardless of whether he likes it or not. He'll get used to it.

Make sure your junk drawer is locked or in a spot he can't get to. Toys should not have dangling strings (cut them off) or batteries unless they are in a child-safe compartment (able to be opened only with a screwdriver). If a toy breaks and has sharp edges, get rid of it. Ditto if it has any small parts that could break off. Toy boxes should have safety hinges and ventilation holes.

Don't let your baby chew on books or other printed material; the ink can be toxic. Do a general wipe-down every day of his toys, because babies spit, dribble and bring up their food, then put their toys in their mouths. Wash what you can wash if they're cloth toys and wipe over the rest.

Be sure that any home he spends time in – childminder's, grandma's – has also been babyproofed, and pay extra attention when friends and relatives come to visit. Be sure that bags are placed up high. Don't leave him alone outside, even for a minute.

SUN PROTECTION

I feel very strongly about protecting your baby from the sun – it's crucial. Too many parents are being irresponsible about this; I've seen too many babies with bright red cheeks cavorting in the water with parents doing nothing. This is not something to take lightly. Sun protection is your moral responsibility. Research shows that even ONE serious sunburn as a child predisposes you to skin cancer as an adult.

Use hypoallergenic baby sunscreen (SPF 30 or higher) on all exposed skin and put it on at least 15 minutes before going out. Find the one that works best for your baby; some can give a rash to babies with sensitive skin. Even waterproof sunscreen needs to be reapplied frequently, especially if he's got himself wet.

Always make sure you put a T-shirt on, even when he's in the water – put it on after you've applied the sunscreen. And don't forget a hat, even in the water! Keep him in the shade as much as possible in warm weather. No matter how much sunscreen you use, if he's turning pink, he's burned, so get him inside!

Also, lead by example yourself. It's no good saying, when he's 15 months, 'Come on, put this on,' when he's never seen you do it yourself.

STIMULATION AND EXPLORATIONS

You're a bit of a stimulation pro now, aren't you? You know what makes your baby laugh, what makes him giggle and grin, as well as what activities he doesn't enjoy. He's developing fast. Not only can he see much better, he's able to reach out for things, pull objects close, shake them, drop them with intent, put them in his mouth. It's a whole different ball game now, so it's important to continue the activities you've been doing while adding more play to develop his motor skills. You'll be getting more feedback from now on, and the interaction you have with your baby will be really rewarding for you as he becomes more adventurous.

PLAY IDEAS
Conversation
Now's the time to begin to encourage a baby's communication skills by having a conversation. Imitate what your baby is saying. If he makes a high-pitched sound, do the same. Soon he'll start to repeat the sounds you make.

This helps develop language, listening and social development. Plus you'll have fun. You don't know what you're saying but you do know what you're saying, and that's what's so beautiful about it.

More tummy time
Your baby's neck muscles are a lot stronger now and are able to support his head. It's important to build that upper-body strength, so a great thing to do is to have him balance on his tummy on a bolster or an inflatable beach ball (with you holding on, of course). Talk to him so he gets engrossed in what you're saying, and he will go longer and longer with that tummy time.

Another thing to do while he's on his tummy is place a plastic ball in front of him and encourage him to stretch out for it. Make it really attractive to him by shaking it a few inches away. If he's got his fingers on it, don't take it away from him, otherwise it's going to be very disheartening because it takes a lot of energy for a baby to reach out and grab that ball. Be aware of the amount of time you spend doing this, because it can be very tiring. Imagine yourself spending three hours in the gym. Need I say more?

A lot of parents feel uncomfortable hearing their child make those determination grunts as they reach for something and go in and rescue. It's important to let him try because it develops the will to keep trying. Nothing was ever achieved by being able to quit easily, so allow your baby to strive for what he wants – unless he gets very frustrated and wails, of course. The reward comes when you see your baby smile with satisfaction from actually having been able to reach out and grab that ball himself: 'It's mine. I've got it!'

Grasp and release

At three to six months, your baby is going to be able to hold things, but not for long. You can help develop his eye–hand coordination and fine motor skills by giving him plastic spoons or keys, Tupperware, rattles and so on to grab on to. Soon he'll drop it, but the more he practises grasp and release, the better he'll get at it.

Superman

It's not safe to throw your baby up into the air and catch him, so I'm not asking you to throw your baby up like a football, but you can lie on your back on the floor with your baby and hold him at arm's length over your head and fly him around. It's great for developing trust as he enjoys that feeling of being up in the air and you supporting him safely.

Bubbles

Who doesn't love bubbles? Bubbles are great because you're able to have so much fun with them and they really do allow your baby to develop eye–hand coordination. Obviously you don't want to drown your baby so he ends up swallowing them.

Bubbles are also a fabulous distraction if your baby's upset.

Dancing ribbons

At this age, I love to take lots of different-coloured ribbons and wave them in front of the baby. By six months, he's able to hold on to the ribbons as they flutter. This also develops eye–hand coordination and allows you to build up those happy memories between the two of you.

Hiding games

Now is also the time for hiding games: take a block and hide it under his blanket for a second with a bit still visible, and then bring it back out. You'll be amazed at how astounded he is. These hiding and throwing-things-down games should go on for many months as your infant learns more and more about object permanence – the fact that things (and people) are there even when you can't see them.

Reading

It's never too soon to start reading to him. He loves the sound of your voice and those infant books with the large colourful pictures are great for his visual stimulation. The more you link pictures with words, the easier it will be for him to do so when he's a toddler. Try the board or cloth ones that are age-appropriate.

Chapter 6
Six to Nine Months

PARENTS' JOURNEY

You may find that, in a way, life up to this point has been relatively convenient because you just breastfed and slept next to your baby and could carry him wherever you wanted to go. Sometime around now, this baby, who has just sat there propped up with pillows like a little Buddha, decides to shock you and disappears. It's a whole different ball game now. He's mobile! For some, it's between six and nine months; for others, later. Whenever it happens, it means you'll be on your feet more, keeping him safe as he makes his rounds. It's going to be harder to contain him while you get done what you need to do.

Once again, you're on a learning curve and will have to adapt. Your routines will have to be flexible enough to take his new mobility into consideration. The good news is that you've got a half-year of experience now, so lots of the routine things, like bathing and changing, should be second nature. In many ways, you're already a pro. Now you're going to apply your experience to a much more excited, rolling and moving baby. For him, it's like, 'Wow! Look where my legs can take me!'

This is when you grow eyes in the back of your head. You wake up one morning, feel two lumps on the back of your head and recognise it's not a headache. There are two eyeballs back there. (If only!)

You're now into a different layer of the Parental Cake of Concern. Up till now you've been concerned about whether he's getting enough food and sleeping through the night. Now it's about keeping him from getting injured or putting something dangerous in his mouth: 'Oh, my God! What's he going to break this time? Is that the dog food he's eating?' Even though you've babyproofed, it will become more apparent how important it is. Many parents don't really get it until now.

This is a lovely stage for parents because there's much more interaction and feedback from the baby. A wonderful rapport builds up because he's mimicking your facial expression and tones. You're able to have semi-conversations. By nine months, he's really come into his own with his personality. You don't just make him laugh any more; he makes you laugh as well.

While you've entered into a new and worrying phase with mobility, at the same time you're definitely more confident in the way you're handling your baby. You've probably weathered some phone calls or visits to the doctor about sniffles or other illnesses. You're making conscious choices about what he wears and who he plays with and may have introduced 'Mummy and me' classes.

Most likely, at some time during this period he'll begin to cut teeth. Oh, my dear, the teething nappy is unlike any other. You would never have thought it possible that your child could ever, ever leave you with such a horrible mess. Where's the gas mask?

Suddenly, your sweet baby may be irritable, and you'll go through another phase of not being able to console him so easily. As a result, you can again feel helpless. When your child is in pain and there's very little you can do, it really hurts. You can't take the pain for him, but you feel it! Your empathy really starts to grow here as you experience, not for the last time, what it's like to feel your child's pain. The best thing you can do is offer your comfort and know that this time will pass.

SOCIALISING TIME

Beginning now, you'll be more active in the world again. It's back to normal really, give or take your baby's routine. This is the time for you and your baby to get out in the world for regular coffee mornings, 'Mummy and me' classes, playdates with other babies in parks, churches and homes, and lunch dates with other babies so they can eat finger food.

GOING BACK TO WORK – CHILDCARE OPTIONS

Some mums will not be a full-time mother and housewife, so the day will come when you'll go back to work. While some mothers go back to work when their babies are younger or older than this, it's often during this time frame that women have to leave their babies, either full- or part-time. This can be a very difficult emotional transition, which mothers often find very challenging. It can feel like you're doing the wrong thing, no matter what the age of your child.

Whatever the reason you go back to work, before you set foot out of that door, you must find someone who you completely, *completely* trust on every, *every* level to leave your baby with. Your first priority is your child. You've got to have absolute trust that you're leaving the most precious thing in your life with someone who can be counted on totally. Otherwise how will you function? You won't. You'll be worrying about your baby!

Because it's such an important decision, I always suggest parents give themselves plenty of time to find the right solution. Begin by taking a realistic look at your circumstances. Will you be going back full- or part-time? Are you on a regular work schedule, or do you often work late or need to go in early? Then, taking into account your finances, make a decision given the available choices. There are basically four options, each with their own pros and cons, including cost:

- family members
- a nanny or nanny-share
- a crèche or daycare centre
- childminder.

Family members

A lot of people have a family member care for their baby, not only because they're family but because it's free. If you choose this option, be sure never to abuse your family. Because you have a need and they're a great solution, there's a tendency to lean on them and then have repercussions down the line. Just because she's your mum or granny, never take her for granted. Let her know all the time how thankful you are and don't take advantage of the situation by asking for more and more time. I've seen single parents in particular take advantage of the situation. Without realising it, they often put too much burden on the co-carer.

You need to be realistic. Can this person really care for your infant all day, every day? Over and over again I've seen family members say, 'Oh, it'll be fine!' and five months down the line realise it's too much for them. I've gone into many families where the grandma says to me, 'I feel bad, but I don't want to look after my grandson because I'm bloody knackered. I can't do it any more.' They feel guilty and are afraid to tell their daughter or son, so I end up doing it.

That's why I think it's important to say, 'Let's start off with two or three months and see how it goes, because I don't want it to be a burden on you.' Then expect that there may be changes. Keep an open relationship – talk about how it's going and how each of you is feeling. Also, if you can afford it, consider giving them a little token of your appreciation. If they don't accept it, then fine.

To avoid any wrinkles, be clear from the beginning about what you're asking your family member to do in terms of routines and so on, and ask if she's willing to follow that. Make no mistake, your mother has earned the right to turn round and say, 'I raised you and your brother and so I know what to do.' But in general, the person you choose has to respect what you two want for your child. If the person you're considering is very controlling and not likely to respect your wishes, you might want to try and find someone else.

I've seen family co-carers take unhealthy liberties, doing everything their way because they know you need them. That's awful, as it puts the parents in a really sticky situation because they desperately need the help. I would encourage you to avoid that situation if at all possible. If you find yourself in it, get out, full stop! Because not only will it damage how you are raising your child, it will tear your relationship with this relative apart. It really will.

Nanny or nanny-share

If you can afford it, nothing beats the one-on-one home care a nanny gives. Nannies are trained and experienced in giving infants 100 per cent of what they need, including stimulating activities, as well as taking care of the needs of any other children. Nanny deals with everything, including being there when your baby is sick, to take her to the doctor, to make organic baby food – in other words to meet the needs of your baby's emotional, mental and social well-being. Nannies are police-checked and know how to do CPR (cardiopulmonary resuscitation). And if you get along well, a nanny will do the local dry-cleaning run too!

Some people with one child find another family with an infant and share a nanny. Either way, it's crucially important to find a great nanny and that means being willing (and able) to pay for it. I always say, 'Pay peanuts, get monkeys.' Simple as that. I find it amazing how people judge the wages of a professional nanny here in the UK. When we walk into Gucci and see a bag, we don't go up to the manager and say, 'That bag for £600, can you knock it down by £200?' Yet a nanny's price is always the subject of dinner-table talk. Your child is the most precious thing in your life! Don't cut corners. We know our stuff.

There are two ways to find a great nanny – word of mouth and reputable nanny agencies. Most of my work was word of mouth. If you get on to the parent network through your antenatal classes or baby groups, you'll meet other parents who can refer you. If that doesn't happen, go the agency route.

There are also two kinds of nannies – those who are formally trained and have certificates, and those who have had a lot of experience and no formal training, like me. If you use an agency, they will do the security procedures. If you're not, then make sure you check all references thoroughly.

When interviewing a nanny, most people hand the baby over because they want to see how their child responds to her, but, to be honest with you, that can be quite tricky. The baby just might be grouchy that day and coincidentally start to cry when the nanny's holding him. Of course you need to pay attention to how she is with children, but it's important that *you* feel good about her too. You need a nanny that you can have a relationship with. Have more than one interview to be sure that the two of you can gel. That person will be coming into your life and spending 12 hours a day or more with your child. It has to be the right person.

Here are some important interview questions:

• What's her experience with newborns?
• What's her opinion on nutrition? Does she cook? You don't need her to be Nigella Lawson, but an ability to put a decent meal on the table is helpful.
• Is she social and outgoing? Is she somebody who's going to connect with other nannies and mums so that your baby will meet other children?
• Is she flexible and able to work around circumstances while maintaining a healthy routine?
• Does she have maturity, energy and a good positive mindset?
• Is she punctual?
• Is she loving and positive? Does she have empathy?
• Will she go on holiday with you if you would like her to?

- Do you share the same beliefs and attitudes about childrearing?
- Do you think you will be able to learn from one another to sustain a wonderful working relationship?
- How long does she want to work for you and how long do you want her for?
- What, if any, is her religion and how does that sit with yours and her work as a nanny?
- If this is a nanny-share, do you think she will be able to give both infants what they need? Is she trained in caring for two infants?

Ultimately you're looking for somebody you can welcome as part of your family because this is an incredibly intimate situation. I've had amazing relationships with the families that I've worked with and keep in contact with them even now, up to 17 years on. Trust your gut instinct. If you feel you need a nanny camera to validate the choice you've made, then you've not made the right choice. We've all seen terrible things on the TV and heard awful stories. If you don't feel sure, bring that woman back in and ask her any question you want, because at the end of the day, it's your child and your decision. If she's not right, then she hasn't got the job.

You can really make up the rules. Are you going to have your nanny on a one- or two-month trial? Is she going to go on holidays with you? What about confidentiality? Try to get all the issues on the table in advance. Write up a contract with the needs of the child and what you expect of the nanny so there are no surprises down the line.

Crèche or daycare centre

If you're considering this option, look at every daycare centre within the vicinity of your home or work. Check out exactly what the staff–child ratio is. Make sure they're licensed so that all the safety issues are watertight. Is it a happy, colourful environment? You don't want a sober, grey centre. Do the other children seem happy? You want to feel good about taking your child there and know that your child's going to be happy. Get references from other parents.

There will be a routine, no doubt, that you can see, but find out about the other basics too:

- Is the place hygienic?
- Do you provide food or do they?
- What age range are the children?
- What activities do they do?
- What educational toys are available?
- Does each baby get individual attention?
- Is there interaction with older children? (I think that's perfectly fine as long as the needs of the younger ones are met and there is a sufficient distinction between who does what, so that the very individual needs of your newborn are being met regardless of the fact that older children are around.)
- What is the educational philosophy of the director?
- Does there seem to be good communication between the people who work there?
- How will they communicate with you about what's happened with your baby that day?

In the end, you want to have the same feeling when you walk into a crèche that you do when you walk into a house that feels great. I would recommend always visiting not just on an open day but also unexpectedly, so that you can see it in action when they're not expecting visitors.

Take into account that with daycare, if one baby gets a cold, they are all going to catch it. Your baby is going to be sicker than other infants who are kept at home because of exposure to all those germs, and generally, you cannot bring a sick baby to daycare so you're going to have to stay home from work if she's ill. New parents often don't expect that, but it is a reality of institutional care.

Childminder

The fourth option is a childminder. This is usually someone who cares for a few babies and/or toddlers in their home, either on their own or with an assistant. I have no problem with that, as long as you make sure the individual is licensed. Licensing ensures that the proper safety precautions are in place, educational toys, child–adult ratios and so on. In other words that she and her house are equipped to provide for the safety and the needs of the children she looks after. Ask to see the licence.

As with a daycare centre, find out all you can about the basics:

- Exactly what does she do with the children all day? Is there a timetable or routine?
- Will you be able to see a diary of what your baby does each day to track her progress?
- Do you provide food or does she? Ask if you can have a weekly sheet of what she feeds your baby if you don't have to bring food in.
- Does she provide nappies?
- Is she open during holidays or will you need to find alternative help?
- What is her sick policy?
- How many children does she look after during the day? At what times? What ages are they? What does the law say about that? How many kids is she authorised to have? She should know the laws and be able to tell you what they are.
- What is her experience and training, and the experience and training of her assistants?
- How recently was her home checked on?

Make sure you also notice what she's like as a person. Just as with a nanny, character is important. A good relationship between the two of you is crucial.

It's your prerogative as a parent to make sure you will feel satisfied about leaving your child. Peace of mind goes a long, long way.

At the end of the day, you must make a choice based on your circumstances, finances, etc. With the information on each option I've given you, I know you'll make the right decision for you and your baby.

How you deal with your own emotions is going to be a process that takes time. There are some things you can do that help. First, don't feel bad if you ring a hundred times a day in the beginning to check on your little one. Tell your caregiver that you will eventually reduce the frequency. Have her keep a log or diary so that you can see what your baby's doing on a daily basis, as this will help you to feel you're not missing out on her growth. Make sure you have someone to talk to about how you're feeling. It's natural to feel sadness and/or guilt for a period of time.

Recognise what you can and cannot change! You cannot change that you need to work, but by recognising that your baby is your priority, you can make work decisions around that. Can you drive her there and back? Can you make sure you're there before she goes to sleep in the evening? Can you avoid business travel during the first year? Can you work one day a week from home?

If after a month or two you still don't feel okay and the situation is affecting you to the point where you're extremely anxious or depressed, then I would definitely question the bigger picture. Is it the place where you're leaving your baby that affects you, or do you and your partner need to start looking at other options so that Mum can work part-time?

I once looked after a baby for six months and the mother came home every day and was fine. Then, over a period of six weeks or so, every evening she came home I thought, 'She's just not quite right.' She seemed vague, and an inner sadness was present. Finally I pulled her aside and said, 'You don't necessarily have to share it with me, but I get the sense you're unhappy.'

She burst into tears, saying, 'I want to stay home with my baby, but I feel so bad because I hired you for a year. I haven't discussed it with my husband, but I know we would be fine financially if I did. Work's not the same now that I have my little one.'

I replied, 'It's your baby. You must do what makes you happy so that you can be the best parent you can, and your baby will be happier too. I'm gone tomorrow!' It was the one time I felt glad to leave, as it's always hard to say goodbye to a family you've built a relationship with.

If you've got a career and a baby, you've got some juggling to do. You can't be a successful businessperson and not put the time in. Something always has to give a little, so tell yourself the truth and work it through.

The first year is all about bonding, so make sure that the time you know you do have with your child is spent in connecting emotionally so that you don't feel withdrawal symptoms, because that's what parents feel when they work – withdrawal symptoms from not being able to bond on a moment-by-moment basis with their child. Make that your priority when you are at home.

The same goes for having fun, fun, fun. You should be enjoying parenthood and spending quality time with your little nipper.

DEVELOPMENTAL OVERVIEW

PHYSICAL DEVELOPMENT

During this time, your baby's head growth is slowing. By eight months, he should weigh somewhere between 13.5–18 lb (6–8 kg). In the seventh month, he can sit on his own for some time, although he usually can't get himself into a sitting position until eight months. Soon, when he topples over, he'll use his arms to catch himself.

He loves to stand while you hold him and bounce up and down, and he can move objects from hand to hand. By the ninth month, he will start using his thumb to hold things and will put his finger into holes.

When he first starts to stand, at about eight months, he won't know how to get back down and you may find him crying for help. Gently bend his knees to get him back down.

When standing, both his tummy and bum stick out so that his back has quite a sway to it. That's perfectly normal until the second year and has to do with his developing sense of balance. His toes may point in or out, but this should also straighten out in the second year. Teach him to fall on his bottom by pushing gently on his tummy to make his knees buckle. He'll go boom. If you smile and laugh, he will too. Help him up and do it again. The idea is to help him learn that he can fall and be okay. Of course make sure he can't hit his head on anything before you do it. And remember, a gentle push.

Typically, around seven to nine months, babies begin to crawl, although some skip this phase altogether and move

> **WHAT YOU MIGHT NOTICE** Around this point of development, you may see some of the following
> - Teeth!
> - Movement!
> - Might start to wave 'hello' and 'goodbye' in response to you.
> - Might begin to experience stranger anxiety.

straight from sitting to walking with no ill effects. Others scoot around on their bums doing what I call the bottom shuffle. Others slither like snakes on their tummies. Many crawl backwards first like little remote-control cars because their arms are stronger than their legs.

In terms of brain development, he's learning to solve his own problems through experimentation, so you'll begin to see him try something a few different ways before giving up. He's learning to set a goal, ignore distractions and persist. And he'll remember what worked before!

TEETHING

Typically this is the period where babies begin to cut their teeth. Beware, breast-feeding mums, when your baby's first tooth comes in – you will probably get bitten. If you cry out, it will probably startle him too. If he keeps doing it, calmly unlatch him and let a few seconds pass before allowing him to latch on again. After a few repeats of this, most babies get the message.

Times can be hard, for you and for him, when he's teething. Teething signs include:

- drooling or dribbling
- hot, itchy, red, swollen gums or a bluish blister (eruption cyst)
- irritability
- chewing on anything and everything
- loss of appetite
- sporadic trouble sleeping
- red cheeks with fine lines that look like a noughts and crosses game
- aching, intermittent cry
- slight fever
- nasty nappies.

There's disagreement as to whether teething causes either fever or diarrhoea. Many medical experts believe something else is going on, perhaps that the stress of teething has lowered the baby's immunity. Check with your doctor or health visitor if you're concerned. It's my opinion that both can be present with teething, and it's nothing that can't be dealt with with lots of TLC, teething aids and Diarolyte, a liquid electrolyte formula that prevents dehydration.

A tooth can take up to two months to break through the gum, and babies can be in acute pain, letting you know it with screams and cries. I swear by Nelson's teething granules, a homeopathic powder that looks like tiny balls, which you put in the baby's mouth. She gnaws it with her gums, a bit like scratching an itch, which can bring some relief.

> **WHEN TO CALL THE HEALTH VISITOR OR DOCTOR**
>
> Has no interest in peek-a-boo by eight months.
>
> •
>
> Doesn't reach for objects by seven months or can't reach for an object with one hand.

Oral gels work, but beware of overuse. Painkillers such as Calpol can also be used. Never give a child aspirin under any circumstances – it is associated with a potentially life-threatening condition called Reye's syndrome, which attacks all the organs of the body, particularly the brain and liver, and can develop from flu, a cold or other illness when aspirin is given.

You can also try teething rings, a cold washcloth, gel packs, or just rub your finger on her gums. Keep her bottom and chin clean and dry, and give lots of cuddles.

Be aware that if your baby bites you, she's not doing it on purpose but because it helps relieve the pressure of teething. You can tell her no biting so she knows not to do it again.

SOCIAL AND EMOTIONAL DEVELOPMENT

At seven months, he is able to remember someone's face. By eight months, he's beginning to make the connection between tones and words and gestures – like bye-bye and waving. He probably loves toys that make a noise when he bangs or shakes them.

By nine months, he can follow simple commands like 'wave bye-bye', point to what he wants and is familiar with the word and tone 'no'. He may want to 'help' with eating now – dipping fingers in and smearing food, holding a spoon or bottle. This may make it harder to feed him, but it's an important step towards eating independently. By nine months, he's able to finger-feed and drink from a sippy cup with your help. He can also now express preferences by pushing away things he doesn't want or grabbing hold of the things he does.

Eight to nine months is when stranger anxiety tends to really kick in. He will probably have a preference for those he already knows, especially the primary carer, and may cry fiercely when a stranger gets close. Give him time to get used to new people by having them approach slowly, and lead by example by showing pleasure at their arrival. You may also find he smiles only for you and other family members he's spent a long time with. By ten months, this stage is usually at its peak.

He may be suddenly afraid of heights or of the bath. You may notice your baby becomes more irritable right before a big jump in development, like crawling. This is perfectly normal. So is resisting sleep, bedtime and naps. Life is just so exciting and challenging!

FEEDING: SOLIDS

In the previous chapter I spoke about how to start introducing very small amounts of suitable baby cereal at six months. Over the next month, you will build on this. Once cereal is well tolerated, I like to make my own homemade organic baby food. It's incredibly easy. Begin with the root vegetables – carrots, sweet potatoes. Wash well, peel, steam until soft, purée in the blender, pour into ice-cube trays and freeze. When it's time for a meal, pop one or two out into a dish, warm in the microwave, stir to get rid of any hot spots, test on your wrist or use one of those temperature-tester spoons that turn a different colour if the food is too hot. Then do fruits – apple and pear sauce, mashed bananas – then other vegetables like peas, courgettes, string beans and avocados, then puréed white meats like chicken and turkey breast, and finally red meat. For meats, cook in milk or steam, then put in the blender. I love my steamer and food processor. When I get going with them, I'm on a roll of food-making heaven. I love the simplicity of being able to give your baby what he needs nutritionally through all the wonderful vitamins in these all-natural purées. Make sure all food is thoroughly cooked and puréed to avoid choking, and if he seems to be having an allergic reaction, get to hospital right away. See the table on page 143 for allergy signs. The more variety he's exposed to when young, the less picky an eater he'll be when older.

Serve dilute baby juices or cooled boiled water along with food to avoid problems with constipation, which often results at the introduction of solids.

The natural sugar in juice can cause bowel movements.

If you use store-bought baby food, stay away from those that contain the words corn syrup, fructose, dextrose or any word ending in -ose – they are all added sugars – or any artificial flavours or colours. Don't feed your baby from the jar; spoon food into a dish first to avoid bacterial contamination from saliva. If you have to feed from a jar, throw away any leftover portion.

Refrigerate any open jars and use within two days or throw away. If you use food from a can, run the can opener through the dishwasher before using, wipe the top of the can and never store leftovers in the can. Store food in plastic or glass containers only. Bacteria breed quickly if food is not stored properly.

By the seven-month mark, you want to be serving solid foods at more

---

GOOD FINGER FOODS
All food should be de-pipped and cut into small pieces (6–9 months onwards)

Fruits: Apples, apricots, avocado, banana (a piece of frozen banana is great for teething babies), mango, melon, nectarine, papaya, peach, pear.

Dried fruit is a good source of iron but don't give too much. Soak it in boiling water to soften it if baby finds it difficult to chew.

Vegetables: Steamed aubergine, green beans, broccoli, sprouts, cabbage, carrots, cauliflower, celery, baby cob, courgettes, peas, potato, swede, sweetcorn, sweet peppers, sweet potato.

Other foods: Bread and rusks dipped in fruit or vegetable purees are good when baby refuses to be spoon-fed.

Miniature sandwiches filled with mashed banana, chopped chicken with fruit chutney, cottage cheese and grated apple, cream cheese and strawberry jam, mashed

sardines and lemon with a teaspoon of tomato sauce.

Start with grated cheese. Once chewing is mastered, move onto chunks and then strips. Avoid strong cheeses like blue, Brie and Camembert. Always make sure it is pasteurised.

Pasta in all shapes and sizes with a vegetable puree and maybe grated cheese on the top.

Strips of chicken are good, especially if it has been cooked in a sauce as they become more tender.

White filleted fish cooked in a sauce is also good.

Braised beef and vegetable casserole or lamb hotpot are great recipes as the meat becomes very soft when cooked for so long.

than one meal now because your baby needs more nutrients. By the end of nine months or so, you may find that his need to breast- or bottle-feed will begin to taper off until it's once in the morning and once in the evening, depending on the decisions you make. This is a natural progression that will help your baby get all the nutrition he requires. If you keep offering breast milk or formula all day, he may not get hungry enough to eat the solids he needs.

Babies at this age still need to eat every three to four hours, so if you are introducing regular mealtimes, be sure to offer snacks mid-morning and mid-afternoon as well. Don't force-feed these snacks.

As your baby's teeth appear and he is able to sit up well in a high chair, you can begin to serve finger foods, which are great for his fine motor skills and pincer grip. Parents may be surprised to learn that babies can use their gums to mash quite a few foods, but keep in mind the food no-nos on page 175 and the choking hazards on page 153. Lamb stew and shepherd's pie are clearly too messy. Cereals, bread and crackers are fine for snacks, but they have too much starch to be given as a meal. You want your baby to be getting vitamins and protein. Try minute pieces of banana, chicken, beef, lamb or pork, cooked carrots, peas or green beans, and cheese, but never the mouldy soft kinds like Brie or blue!

Keep to foods that are au naturel – no artificial colours or flavourings. Again, introduce foods one at a time and make sure you offer variety. Don't keep pushing just the apple sauce. A new food every week or so is a good pace. If he doesn't like something, try serving it for a couple of days. If he still rejects it, try it again in a week or so.

SLEEPY-TIME FOODS

Did you know that certain foods, like oatmeal and turkey, tend to create sleepiness? It's due to the presence of tryptophan, a chemical that produces drowsiness. That's why at Christmas we fall asleep at the table.

He will eat a nice portion of food now at each feeding. Generally children know when they are full, especially when they're young. Trust him to show you when he's had enough. Also be aware that babies eat in spurts – don't expect him to consume the same quantity each meal.

At around the nine-month mark, you can begin to serve liquids in a sippy cup. Plastic no-spill sippy cups with no handles and a soft spout are great to begin with. I suggest you offer water. If you offer juice, even diluted, babies quickly prefer it because it's sweet. There's no need to encourage a sweet tooth!

Make sure your baby is wearing a bib, which will save you from washing clothes after each meal. I love the big plastic ones that have a scoop bottom because I get a great kick out of watching babies concentrate on picking food out of it and feeling pleased with themselves for achiev-ing it.

At around nine months, he'll watch you and copy you. As you open your mouth to eat, he'll open his: 'Here comes the choo-choo, in it goes, bye-bye.'

Make sure you don't have toys on his high-chair tray while feeding; it makes the whole process much harder if he's trying to play. Give him a plastic spoon to hold, even if all he does is bang it on the table while the other spoon goes in.

FIRST-YEAR FEEDING

Don't feed the following to a baby under a year old:

- **Sugar, corn syrup or honey:** babies don't need any added sugar, and honey and corn syrup contain botulism spore, which can kill infants.
- **Salt:** too hard on a little one's kidneys and so not to be added.
- **Eggs or products with eggs:** egg whites may cause allergies. Cooked yolks may be given once the baby is established into a good mixed feeding routine, usually between eight and nine months.
- **Unpasteurised juices:** can cause illness or death.
- **Citrus fruits:** too acidic.
- **Shellfish:** can cause allergies and is an acquired, mature taste.
- **Seeds and nuts, including peanut butter:** can cause allergies and are extreme choking hazards.
- **Tomatoes and strawberries:** often cause allergies.
- **Wheat or corn products:** often cause allergies. Should never be given to babies under the age of six months.
- **Cow's milk:** too much protein. Should never be given to babies under the age of six months.

Eventually he'll figure out what to do with it. Yoghurts in pots are good for little ones to play around with as they are small and easy to hold and dip a spoon into.

SETTING FIRM GROUND

SLEEPING: SOLID SLEEP

By now you have a few things in place for a solid sleep routine: he's in his cot, in his own room, or separated by some kind of light and noise divider from others, and on solid foods.

It's important that you place him in his cot awake, otherwise you start to create bad habits. If your child gets used to falling asleep in your arms, then when he wakes up he'll become very fretful because you're no longer there.

By now, your baby will be awake more of the time. That's wonderful, but you need to make sure he has two sleeps during the day – one in the morning and one in the afternoon, lasting between an hour and two hours each.

At around eight months, his sleep might start to be disrupted – you'll find him testing boundaries regarding sleeping around now, and again at 13 months.

CONTROLLED-CRYING TECHNIQUE

Now that he's on solid foods, he'll be able to go to sleep on his own and stay asleep through the night. The importance of getting your baby to sleep through the night is crucial if everybody's going to avoid being sleep-deprived.

So you don't end up going in to comfort your child dozens of times, use my Controlled-Crying Technique. I've used it to great success with six-month-old babies up to toddlers. Use it first for naps, then night-time.

You need a timer and a strong resolve. The first time he cries, you go in, reassure and then leave. Wait five minutes and if he's still crying, go back in and repeat the routine. Then wait ten minutes and return if necessary, then 20. In other words, you double the time each time. Soon you'll have a baby who can soothe himself to sleep without you.

When you go in to say, 'shhhh', just rest your hand on him without eye contact and then leave. Do not pick him up or it will lead him to think he's getting out of bed. Some babies will cry and start to gag. If he throws up, take him from his cot, clean him up and place him back in. Then start the technique again.

If you've got a baby who's still in your room because you don't want to put him with your six-year-old, use the same technique, but with you in the room. If he wakes in the night crying and you are lying in bed, wait the five minutes and then go over, lay him down and say, 'Shhhh.' Then go to ten minutes, just as I describe above. It is going to be harder because he can see you and he'll be screaming like nobody's business right near you, but if you keep at it, he will learn.

Whether he's in your room or not, it is the consistency of the technique that makes it work, along with making sure that he's getting lots of love, attention and stimulation during waking hours. If he is getting all he needs from you during the day, this technique of active ignoring is not neglect. Rather, it is teaching him in a healthy way to soothe himself to sleep, and that's an important process for every child to learn.

CORNERSTONE ROUTINE 6–9 MONTHS

This routine shows a baby who has reached the stage of being comfortable with solids: you should work up to this point and adapt it as described below as the months go by. Time all feeds from when the baby begins to feed.

7am	Breastfeed 20–40 minutes or bottle-feed 6 oz (170 ml)	A good milk feed in the morning is vital and sets the baby up for the day. As you move through this period you may drop some of the daytime milk feeds: if so you should increase this feed to 9 oz (255 ml).
8.30am	Breakfast	As your baby gets more established on solids, work up to giving her a solid breakfast consisting of, for instance, a good portion of baby muesli mixed with milk or pureed fruit. Afterwards she should have a nap of about an hour.
10.30am	Breastfeed 20–40 minutes or bottle-feed 6 oz (170 ml)	As the months go by, you can gradually cut down and then cut out this milk feed.
1pm	Lunch	As you start solids, lunch might be a couple of spoonfuls of vegetable or fruit puree, working up to about two ice cubes' worth as the baby gets comfortable with solids. Try to introduce any new foods at this meal as it gives your baby a chance to digest them throughout the afternoon. You will want to start introducing protein and especially iron-rich foods. By 7 months you should be giving at least one portion of protein a day. You can also start to introduce a dessert to this meal as your baby approaches nine months: as she starts to get on the move she will need lots of energy. Start to encourage finger foods. Make sure you also offer liquid in the form of water or very well-diluted juice.

2pm	Breastfeed 20–40 minutes or bottle-feed 8 oz (225 ml)	After this feed the baby should have a good nap of about two hours.
5pm	Tea	Once your baby is happy eating solids make sure they get another good meal at this time of day, made up of a good nutritious mixture of vegetables, carbohydrates and perhaps more protein. You might find that as the months go by you need to start offering this meal a little a bit later to make sure that the baby is hungry enough to eat all he needs.
6pm	Breastfeed 20–40 minutes or bottle-feed 8 oz (225 ml)	Milk is still crucial to your baby's development and your baby will need another milk feed before his bedtime routine. Bathe him, brush his teeth, give him a story or a song, and settle him for the night. You should now encourage your baby to sleep through the night, using controlled crying if necessary, so it is important that his tummy is full enough to carry him through until morning.

PARENTCRAFT

DRESSING

Remember my rule-of-thumb about working with your baby when you're dressing him. The older he gets, the more he's not going to want to lie down, so once he can sit up on his own, don't lie him down to get him dressed all the time. Instead let him sit up and put the top over his head. Change the scenery as well. Don't always get him dressed in the same place and the same position. You'll find you get less resistance.

BATHING

Once your baby can sit up confidently, he can graduate to one of those ring seats in the big bathtub, with you holding on and never leaving for a second, of course. Once he's a solid sitter, you can just place him in the big tub.

From about six months on, bathing is not just about hygiene, but about having fun and developing his confidence with water. Of course, toys you wind up, toys that squeak and toys that splash water help bathtimes become something that he relishes, not just part of his routine.

Here are a few tips for making it a fun and safe experience:

- Make sure the room is nice and warm. If it's slightly humid, it helps babies with breathing problems and counteracts dry air.
- Get everything you need for when he gets out of the bath ready.
- Put down non-slip bathmats inside and outside the bath.
- The less confident you feel, the less water you should have. You never want a swimming pool, but you can graduate to a bit more water as you get used to the awkwardness of bending over and holding on as you wash.
- Test the water to make sure it's not too hot or cold.
- Always hold on – you don't want him to slip.
- Consider getting a guard for the tap so he won't hurt his head on it.
- Use liquid soap and shampoo, because babies have been known to choke on bits of bar soap.

- Get him used to having a sponge on his head with very gentle water trickling down.
- Keep a big towel by your side to wrap him in when he comes out.

NAPPY-CHANGING

Sometimes, beginning at around eight months, babies will stick their hands in the poo when you're changing them if you're not fast enough to catch them. By this time in their lives, they are usually pooing three times a day – morning, afternoon and night. If you pay attention, you'll minimise the mess. No matter what, stay calm. Just wash his hands and say in a clear voice, 'That's poo-poo. Not on your hands, stay in nappy.'

At about this time, he may resist getting his nappy changed – it's taking up too much of his day and he'd rather be playing. Find a good distraction. Give him something to hold on to and talk to him at the same time.

DINING OUT

As he gets into solid food and becomes more active, eating out with your baby will be messier and more challenging. The key is to create a fun experience for you and your child. Go for a family-friendly restaurant and keep it short and sweet. If you make it fun, you'll feel competent enough to do it again.

Bring a few things for him to play with – blocks, books, finger puppets, and of course there's always the 'I drop it and you pick it up game.'

Play it by ear. You might want to feed him before and then let him have a few finger foods at the table. Remember about time. An eight-month-old cannot sit for as long as an adult, so don't expect to have a three-course meal. By now he's on a very consistent routine as well, so you know you only have a certain amount of time before he starts to get tired. However, there's no reason why he can't get out of the high chair and into the stroller and lie back if he really starts to droop. Beware of the crayons they often give out at family restaurants, because of course he's going to want to pop them in his mouth. A definite no-no.

HARNESSING TROUBLE

Your little one's more mobile now, so be sure to strap him into any pushchair, supermarket trolley or high chair. You may be encountering the 'No, no' shaking of head, making himself as stiff as a board, and temper tantrums, whether on car rides, plane flights or shopping trips. Those screams can be incredibly stressful for you. Start by figuring out if he's wet or hungry, or whether something's pinching him. Is he too hot? Too cold? If you've taken care of all those needs and it's being confined that's the problem, try distractions – a toy, a song, jiggle the seat, try peek-a-boo while strapping him in. Make sure he has enough of a play before getting into the car.

Whatever you do, remain calm. She's too young to reason with. Sometimes these moments simply have to be endured while you do what you need to do. Above all, don't give in to 'What kind of parent will everyone think I am if my child is screaming?' It doesn't matter that everyone's looking. Here's one of your first chances to ask yourself, 'What kind of parent am I?' One that's not going to do the right thing because other people are looking? It's your job to do the right thing for your child, whether she likes it or not, and whether it creates a scene or not. There are some crucial things she's not going to like, but which are non-negotiable. Harnesses are one!

BABYPROOFING

Now that she's in motion, make sure you've safety-proofed the house adequately, following my recommendations in the Babyproofing section on page 58. In the blink of an eye, she can tumble down the stairs, put a finger in an electric socket, choke on a button battery or drown in an inch of water.

When your baby's in motion, it's a fine balance between creating a safe environment and going overboard. You need to decide what you're going to get out of the way and what you're going to teach your child about. For instance, some people say, 'We've got a cat, and the cat is always going to be there, and the cat food's always going to be there. So we're going to teach our baby, "Come away from there – that's the cat food" instead of putting it out of reach.'

This stage is about recognising what things you want to keep around and teach your child to avoid, and what things you're going to take away until he's older. If you can make the distinction, then you're halfway there, but don't expect to keep a palace. After all, you have kids and you don't want to keep telling them, 'No.'

STANDING HAZARDS

Now he can stand, make sure the cot and changing table are not by a window as this is very dangerous. First, you have this immobile baby, and then, all of a sudden, it's like, 'Da-dum! Mission Impossible!' Off he goes! Changing him on a pad on the floor eliminates the danger.

This is the time to take away mobiles, too, so that he can't stand up, pull it down and get tangled. Lower the cot mattress to the lowest setting so he can't fall out easily, and remove any large toys he can stand on to boost himself up and out. Get rid of bumpers now, because he can stand on those to get out too.

CRAWLING HAZARDS

Get down on the floor for a crawling baby's view of the world to make sure you've eliminated all dangers – tippy vases or lamps on coffee tables, your favourite knick-knacks, tablecloths, top-heavy chairs and the like. This is about keeping not only your baby safe, but your things as well. As your baby becomes mobile, he will want to explore his world as much as possible, and you don't want to have to worry about Aunt Tilly's prize-winning pot getting

NANNY NO-NO
Animal avoidance: There are a number of animals that babies should not come in contact with because they have been found to carry salmonella and other dangerous illnesses:

• baby chicks and ducklings
• toads and frogs
• turtles
• lizards
• snakes.

smashed, not to mention your dear little one getting hurt. He's not going to think, 'Ohhhh! That's a Wedgwood! I better leave that one alone! Let me go and just touch the one from Ikea!' He is not aware of how hard you worked to buy that ornament on the side table. He'll have it down like he's knocking coconuts at the fair. I've also seen people who have their wines in racks ready to pull out. Pull them out he will. Put anything you consider precious away and put the household stuff in appropriately high places!

Put his books and toys on low shelves and move the things you want to preserve to the top ones. Make sure furniture's safe against the wall so your baby can't pull it over on himself. Be sure to keep the chest of drawers and cupboard doors closed or you may find them being used as climbing devices. You can get wedges that fit over doors so they never really close and he can't jam his fingers in them. They look like big foamy Cs.

You can buy edge and corner cushions to avoid bumps and bruises, and use foam tape around the edges of glass tables. Block off furniture that she can crawl under and get stuck. When babies start to crawl, they're not like cats; they don't have whiskers to determine the width of something, so they go in somewhere and can't get back out again. Sometimes babies will crawl forward and then realise, 'I don't know how to reverse to get back out!' You have to pull them out, which always makes me laugh.

Keep appliances unplugged as much as possible and don't allow cords to dangle. Once your child is mobile, be cautious of safety hazards – such as open doors and windows, and stairs.

Place guards in front of fireplaces, and remove space and kerosene heaters. Tie up cords to blinds and curtains so he can't reach them, or use a cleat in the wall to make sure nothing's dangling. Hanging cords are a strangulation hazard.

Be even more careful about pets now that he can move. His crawling can scare your cat or dog and cause aggression, so make sure you're always around your child and pet.

IN THE BATHROOM

Consider installing a safety latch on your toilet lid so that a baby that's fascinated with the toilet can't fall in. Toilets are dangerous because babies are top heavy – if they lean over, they do tumble in.

Keep make-up, medicines, toothpaste, razors, tweezers, curling irons, hairdryers and the like out of reach. Beware where you put your cosmetic and perfumed goodies – to your little one, they look like coloured drinks in bottles. Because they're all bright and vibrant, babies will put them in their mouths.

Perfumes, because they have alcohol, are particularly poisonous. Train yourself to put them out of reach and close the bathroom door behind you.

IN THE KITCHEN

Make sure the rubbish bin has a tight lid on it. Keep all vitamins out of reach – iron poisoning is the most common cause of infant poisoning death. Don't let him play with the knobs on the stove and be mindful of the oven door as it gets hot. The same goes for the iron and ironing board. And if you have pets, the food and water bowls are tempting targets for a crawling baby. Be sure to put them somewhere he can't get to. As for cat-litter boxes, you definitely don't want him getting into that!

Most burns of children aged six months to two years come from the spilling of hot liquids and foods, so keep your little one in a safe spot in the kitchen, as far away from ovens and appliances as possible. I advise putting him in a baby gym next to a little wicker basket full of his toys to occupy him while you're cooking. At eight and nine months, babies need engaging all the time.

If he's on the loose, put him in a safe corner with toys, and if he crawls to you, make sure you take him back out of harm's way. Apart from the safety reasons, putting the high chair next to the stove is a problem because you'll be giving your baby food to keep him quiet while you're not able to give him attention. This sets up a link between comfort and eating. Don't pacify with food!

NEVER OUT OF SIGHT

I hope I've helped you become aware of the kind of things you need to be vigilant about. Once your eyes are open, you're never again going to think, 'I can sit back and let my baby crawl all over the house by himself.' Know exactly what's in every room that may be a danger. At this stage, your child shouldn't be anywhere by himself for so long that he could, for instance, go to the washing machine, undo the door, and get in. Basically, if he's crawled off the radar screen, Mum and Dad, go get him.

STIMULATION AND EXPLORATIONS

Ready, world, here comes baby! This time is about continuing to support fine and gross motor development so that crawling and walking come along nicely, as well as continuing aural and visual stimulation.

PLAY IDEAS
Keep talking!

Take the sounds he's making – 'da, da', for instance – and turn them into words for him: Daddy, bottle, etc. He may not say his first recognisable word until a year or so, but he understands your tone much earlier.

Narrate what you're doing as you care for him. Be sure your language is simple and concrete. Describe what's happening: 'Now we're taking a bath. Does the water feel good? Here comes the soap . . .' Label everything as you use it: 'Want the spoon now?' Pause as if you were having a conversation with an adult and wait for a response. You may get only a 'gaga', but he's learning the give and take of conversation, and your expectation that he will speak will encourage him to do so.

Footie

Okay, I'm not promising you that your baby is going to turn into the next David Beckham, but I don't know any baby of this age who doesn't love a game of footie. Hold your baby securely in front of you, position his legs on top of a ball and make it roll across the floor. This works on eye–foot coordination and gross motor skills. Of course it's not going to be until he's two, two and a half years old that he's actually going to be able to kick the ball by himself. You're providing the muscle power, and he's getting to kick his legs, gurgle and enjoy the experience.

Head and shoulders

When babies are born, they have no sense that they are separate beings from their mothers. There's no conscious thought process involved, but the more they move around, the more they start to realise they are their own person.

To reinforce this, you can play peek-a-boo in the mirror and identify body parts: 'Here is Mummy's eye; here is Max's eye.' Or just touch a body part and name it, or sing the old favourite 'Head, shoulders, knees and toes'. Babies love it.

A soft landing

When you're playing with your child and he starts sitting up by holding his hands in front of him looking like a tripod, then lifts his hands up and starts to fall over, it's important to let this happen, at the same time cushioning the fall with your hands so he doesn't hurt himself. This will ensure he doesn't feel scared. His balance will soon start improving and it won't happen nearly so often.

Obstacle course

Isn't it funny the way your baby is beginning to crawl? Some babies bottom-shuffle backwards. They remind me of little wind-up plastic babies, going over things rather than round. They just go forwards or backwards. What fun!

You can encourage crawling by placing something he's interested in right in front of him so that he will crawl over to it. Get down on the floor with him and let him crawl over you. As he gets more adept, create obstacle courses with small pillows, sofa cushions and boxes. Put him at one end of a tunnel and your face at the other end so he can crawl through it to you as you encourage him.

Add peek-a-boo by hiding behind an object. Make sure you are constantly with him while doing this because he can get stuck under a box or covered by a cushion, which can be frightening as well as dangerous. And be sure to pick everything up when the game is over so he doesn't accidentally get trapped.

'Until now, everything you've been doing has involved you. It's important to develop the baby's ability to play solo.'

Puppet shows

As babies reach the nine-month mark, I like to put on finger puppets and entertain my little charges. Add music and you can put on a musical show. It allows you to interact with your baby on a social level, and because he's more in tune with his visual tracking, he's able to see exactly what's in front of him and grasp at it.

Food fun

You can play all sorts of games while feeding. One of my favourites is where the spoon is a train and you pretend you don't know where it's gone as the baby engulfs it, relishing in the delight that he's swallowed it and you don't know where it is. He'll love your surprised face.

A drawer of his own

As your baby becomes mobile, he's going to get curious about the world around him, so be sure to have a dedicated place with safe objects in it for him to explore. Fill one of the bottom kitchen drawers with lots of Tupperware, plastic cups and measuring spoons for him to rummage through to his heart's content.

His pincer grasp will develop around eight months, so he'll love to pick up objects using his thumb and forefinger. Give him an object like a set of measuring spoons and a large container from his drawer and show him how to drop them in the container and how to take them out again. He'll want to do it over and over again. Remember, repetition is the name of the baby game.

Keep a set of stacking cups in there too. He'll love to bang them together and hear the noise. He's becoming aware that he can create that noise for himself.

Old-fashioned games

I love all those games we played with our grandmothers and they played with their parents, like:

- Ride a cock-horse to Banbury Cross, where you've got your child on your lap and you're bouncing him up and down
- Humpty Dumpty sat on the wall, where you have him fall . . . (while still holding on, of course)
- Twinkle, twinkle, little star
- Incy Wincy Spider
- Row-row-row your boat, where you hold his hands and rock back and forth.

All these games allow you to connect physically with your child in a way that is fun and exciting as well as good for his development.

Activity toys

I'm a firm believer in activity boards, baby-gym rings and pop-up toys, starting between six and nine months. They help develop his fine motor skills and discover cause and effect: push this and the duck goes quack. The pop-ups also allow him to begin to understand object permanence. In order to help him learn the amount of pressure he needs to put on the button so that it actually works, just put your hand over his and say, 'Press down,' or 'Flip this,' whatever movement it is.

I love activity boards because they allow your baby to explore on his own. Up until now, everything you've been doing has involved you. It's important to develop his ability to play solo.

Although he may start fussing as soon as you put him down, it's important for him to get comfortable sitting on his own, propped up with cushions, for a moment. Try settling him in a baby gym with an activity board while you're preparing lunch or grabbing a quick coffee. You can stay close and talk to him so that he knows that you're there. Gradually increase your distance and the duration of time so that by the time he's nine months, you can get up from the sitting room to go and put in a load of washing because you know he's going to be okay on his own (in a babyproofed environment, of course).

Baby-gym rings are great when you have another parent and baby around as you can put both babies into the ring, where they can have fun with the activities and begin social development at the same time. Have you ever watched two young babies together? First they don't notice one another; then they look very intensely. Then you start to see them babble and touch each other. 'Hello, you.' It's absolutely delightful to see.

The big, wide world

As your baby hits the nine-month mark or so, the outside world becomes a fascinating place: trees rustling, branches swaying, the sound of birds. You'll get to a point sometime now when your baby will want to be turned round in the pram to look outwards. You'll know it because he'll start to protest when he's being placed in it. Don't take it personally. Your baby has looked at your face six million times and loves you but now wants to see everything beyond Mummy. He's ready to start interacting with the rest of the world.

Chapter 7

Nine to Twelve Months

PARENTS' JOURNEY

You're much more of a relaxed mum and dad now, right? You know your child well, and your child knows you. At this stage he's probably just saying a few syllables, but his body language and facial expressions speak volumes, and you know exactly what he's communicating. You also have a mental log of what works and what your child needs. All of this put together is making life so much easier.

For example, you may be sitting with a friend while your baby is in the pram kicking his feet and laughing. Then you see a little bit of anxiousness and his facial expression changes. Being able to read his body language, and recognise that he's been sitting there for 20 minutes while you've been talking, allows you to make a very clear decision about what to do next. Out for a bit of attention and then down for a nap.

Whereas before you might have panicked because of your lack of experience and run to him at every little whim and cry, now you know that you can wait a bit and it won't hurt. In fact, it will help teach him patience, eventually. It's important for both parents and baby to learn that you're not immediately at their beck and call, and is especially critical for mothers who have older children because you're going to need to find a balance as your baby enters the toddler years while you're also looking after older children.

You've done a good job of reading and following my advice. Now, rather than following the text to the letter, you're starting to ad lib because you know your baby better than anyone else. That makes sense. You have your way, and other parents have theirs. That's okay. Don't let competitive parents who seek to be always right cause you to doubt yourself.

You should be very, very proud of yourselves. Parenting is a rewarding job, but the rewards are not given through raises or promotions. Hopefully, your family and friends have been telling you how well you've been doing and have continued to be supportive.

Think of all you've given your baby. You may not have the 300-thread-count baby sheets or the latest toys, but your baby has relaxed, energised parents because you have a consistent sleep routine. Your baby has great social skills because you've been an interactive mother who has made the effort to meet up with other mums and babies. And your baby has confident parents whom she trusts.

Make sure that your life is not all about the baby. You may look at him and see that he's very happy and well looked after, but how about you? It's important to focus on yourselves too because your baby's not there to fill a void in your life. Your baby's there because the pair of you decided to raise a human being.

What things are you doing for yourself? Be sure you have goals for yourself even if it's just going to the gym twice a week or meeting up with a friend for lunch or doing some work that you have been wanting to do. Now's the time to start learning to juggle raising your child with other things that are important to you. I disagree with that old saying that once we have kids our life stops. Your priorities change, of course, and there are certain things that you don't do any more, but your life can go on.

Some mums, for instance, find that balance when their babies are this age by going swimming and putting their child into a crèche before taking them to their own swim class. They get some exercise

> 'Your baby has great social skills because you've been an interactive mother who has made the effort to meet up with other mums and babies.'

and release stress, as well as having fun with their baby afterwards – and the good thing about leaving your child in a crèche is that it gives him a chance to interact with other children as well as adults other than yourself. It helps his social development and object permanence (the object being you – you go and will come back). It's healthy for him, it's healthy for you, and it's only an hour at the most. And if your child is really crying, the staff can get hold of you in a heartbeat.

NEW ROLES

By this stage, you're leading by example whether you realise it or not. Your baby is now watching and learning from your every move: how you sit and eat, how you react to situations, your body language. This watching and imitating will go on for years. He's increasingly more aware of the environment, which includes people and feelings, but also sights and sounds. As adults, we take these things for granted, but at this age they can be terrifying. Your job is to reassure him and help him make sense of the world.

I remember looking after a little girl who freaked out every time I pulled the plug out of the bath because of the noise the water made as it gurgled down the hole. I told her in a sweet tone that that was where the little people lived and the water went down to make sure that they had their baths too. The thought of these little people made it okay, not that she fully understood me, being so young, but my calming voice and letting her know that everything was all right did the trick.

So it's your job to become aware of what might be frightening your baby and reassure him. Aeroplane noises, fireworks, toilets flushing – he's becoming consciously aware of these now, and how you deal with them is important. My advice is – validate what he's going through (in other words, acknowledge his fear) and pacify him, but also give a very short and simple reassurance and move on.

Your baby's mobility again accelerates during this period. He can think ahead a bit now, but not about the end result, so you're still going to be up on your feet and rescuing him a lot. It's also the time for a whole new parenting skill: watching your child bump into things when crawling and falling down as he learns to walk. You wish the whole world were made out of rubber, so he'd bounce back without a scratch. You don't want him to fall and hurt himself, but you know that you have to let him experiment in order for him to grow.

'Try not to let your concerns about what other people might think influence the decisions you make for your child.'

You need to learn to step back, because your fear and upset is contagious. Over and over again I've seen kids fall because their parents yell,

'Watch out.' Or they fall and they're fine until they see that the parent is worried, and then the wailing starts. This is not to say that you shouldn't validate that your baby's fallen over, but do it in a calm manner.

Indeed, this is a time when you need all the calm you can muster, because babies at this age do fall and get big egghead bruises, and then you sit there worrying what other people are going to think about you as a parent. That's a place you really don't want to go. Just deal with what you need to deal with – your own family, your own baby. Try not to let your concerns about what other people might think influence the decisions you make for your child. That's what being a confident parent is about – standing sure in your own belief in yourself.

THE EMOTIONS OF WEANING

You may have done it sooner, but at some point around now you're probably going to wean your baby. From the emotional point of view, some women can feel very sad about the end of this intimate connection, so don't do it till you're ready.

One thing that helps is to recognise that by weaning you're taking your bond to a different level, where you can still have intimacy with your child. You can still have quiet times, those times when it's just you and him. He's still dependent on you; it's just not about your breasts (if you've got any left, looking at those chicken fillets that you're going to have to put in your bra!). Your baby will always be your baby, but now he's heading towards toddlerhood. Your focus here should be on continuing to do your best as a parent to help your child reach healthy milestones.

I recently helped a woman wean her 14-month-old and it was completely liberating for her and her child. She hadn't wanted to give up breastfeeding because of a lack of intimacy with her husband. Now that's changed too.

DEVELOPMENTAL OVERVIEW

PHYSICAL DEVELOPMENT

By ten months, your baby knows his own name, responding by turning his head, moving towards you or making sounds. He's become a master copycat, mimicking the gestures of those around him. He has become capable of a sequence of actions – for instance, picking up a clothes peg and putting it into a pail and then taking it out again.

By 11 months, he'll probably be able to 'couch-walk' – walk while holding on to furniture. Sometime soon he'll also stand on his own and then take his first step or two without holding on, which will result, no doubt, in great parental delight and applause, which encourages him to keep on trying. You'll find yourself saying 'no' more often as you pull him away from potentially dangerous or messy situations and physically remove him to more safe locations.

Around 12 months, he also begins to understand the names of body parts (especially if you name them when you bath or change him). By one year, he may understand up to 100 words, although he may not say more than a few – or none at all – at this point. As long as he's making sounds that vary in pitch and intensity, you can be sure his first words aren't far away. Feeding himself becomes easier, including drinking from a sippy cup and getting that spoon in his mouth.

By his first birthday, he has typically tripled his birth weight and is 28–32 inches (70–80 cm) tall. (But remember, it's your baby's growth rate that's important, not these specific numbers.) He'll be able to stack blocks, put things inside others (nesting containers) and even do one-piece puzzles. (The ones with big knobs on them are good for helping develop the pincer grip, which is the ability to grasp something with thumb and forefinger.) He'll also be able to eat with his fingers and 'help' you dress him by putting out an arm or leg.

> **WHEN TO CALL THE HEALTH VISITOR OR DOCTOR**
>
> Doesn't crawl by 12 months.
>
> •
>
> Can't stand when supported by ten months.
>
> •
>
> Says no single words, like 'Mama' by 12 months.
>
> •
>
> Does not look for objects that you hide while he watches.
>
> •
>
> Doesn't use gestures, like shaking head or waving, by 12 months.

SOCIAL AND EMOTIONAL DEVELOPMENT

During this time, he starts to look to you for what to do when he's unsure. He wants you to indicate with a smile or a word or a nod that what he's doing is okay. This shows he's developing both self-consciousness and the awareness of social approval and disapproval.

He will most likely cry when you leave, and will show a preference for particular toys. At some point in this phase, he will figure out that the baby in the mirror is himself.

By 11 months, you may begin to see parallel play, meaning playing next to, but not with, another child. He may all of a sudden become afraid of certain

WHAT YOU MIGHT NOTICE

As your baby begins to move towards the year mark, you might notice him:
• Beginning to understand his name.
• Playing games such as block stacking.
• 'Couch walking' or 'cruising' round furniture.

objects or sounds, like thunder or the vacuum cleaner. If, as with thunder, you can't prevent it, comfort him and stay as calm as you can. Your emotions are contagious.

His sense of humour really kicks in now. He knows what makes you laugh and you'll have a lot of fun together. The downside is that he's going to be testing the boundaries – but not in a way that's defiant. It comes from being curious. If he's doing something he shouldn't, you need to begin to establish boundaries through a low tone of voice and a facial expression that shows you're not happy.

You'll begin to see just what a little actor you've given birth to. There should be a baby Oscar night rewarding how babies try to trick us with little coughing noises and head shaking. Most parents are quite surprised when I tell them that their baby is trying to pull a fast one. 'I never knew babies were that clever!' Oh, yeah – believe.

A classic example is when you give him something to eat that he doesn't like and he makes a sound like the throttle of a car trying to start, making out that the food is choking him. Of course you need to check to see if he is choking, but usually it's only because he doesn't want that particular food. It's a response to change. Like adults, most babies want to stick to what they know, and some are more reluctant to embrace change than others.

You'll find his emotions are all over the place during this stage. He's high one moment and then the next moment bursts into tears, and this all happens very quickly.

LEAVE-TAKING TECHNIQUES

As separation anxiety sets in, it can be extremely upsetting when your baby begins to wail and cling when you try to leave. You may feel guilty or suffocated by his constant clinging, wishing he would just leave you alone! Remember that this phase will end, and try to make your leave-taking as calm as possible. Here are some effective leave-taking techniques:

- Separations are the hardest when your baby is hungry, tired or sick. As much as possible, leave after he's been fed and had a nap, and avoid separations when he's sick.
- Have the other caretaker create a distraction with something like a toy or a bath. Say, 'Bye-bye,' and leave calmly: 'Mummy's going now.'
- Practise by telling him you're going into another room and will be back in one minute, then go for one minute and return. He'll learn that you do return.
- If you're taking him somewhere else to stay – someone's house, or a daycare centre perhaps – stay for a few minutes before announcing you're leaving and will be back soon. Give a cuddle and go.
- Above all, remember that the wails subside as soon as you leave. They are his attempt to get you to stay. Once he has understood that that fails, he'll soon get involved with the caretaker.

He will also begin to display separation anxiety, meaning he has figured out that there is only one of you and he wants you all the time! Babies have no sense of time, so when you leave, they have no idea of when you might be back. Separation anxiety usually begins at ten months and appears again at about 18 months.

By 12 months, he'll be able to express love to people and objects, with kisses and sounds that indicate affection.

As he hits the one-year milestone, he'll begin to want to do things for himself – feed or put things in a sorter. The more you can allow him, the more his abilities and patience will grow.

SETTING FIRM GROUND

By this time, your baby should be firmly established in his feeding and sleeping routines.

FEEDING

As he approaches one, you can introduce a variety of different foods, though you should continue to avoid salt, sugar, peanuts and honey. Make a food plan that is balanced and nutritious. Try to make sure your baby gets at least one serving of protein a day, together with a good amount of both carbohydrate and fruit or vegetables at each meal. You should also include full-fat meals such as cheese or yoghurt as your baby gets on the move and starts to use up more energy. Try to include iron-rich foods as often as possible, and don't forget to give enough liquids.

By one year, he should be able to use a spoon to dig out what he wants. He'll eat with his fingers, mostly, so be prepared for mealtimes to be a slow and messy but fun process. Feeding himself helps his fine motor coordination and pincer grip, and the more he practises getting spoon and hand to mouth, the better he'll get.

Yoghurt is good for practising because it stays well on the spoon. You're there at this point to provide appropriate foods in appropriate-sized pieces as I described in the Chapter 6 section, to watch for choking, to help when needed and to clean up afterwards.

Babies at this age will try anything, so start teaching good eating habits and proper portion sizes through your choices. Get clued up, buy books, read all about it. Obesity and type 2 diabetes are on the rise. Do your part in curbing these epidemics!

I am a great believer in strapping babies into their

FOOD TRICKS

One way to help him learn to use a spoon and eat unfamiliar things is to put a bit of new food in yoghurt. Make each spoonful less yoghurt and more of the new food until he's got it.

high chairs to eat meals on a schedule. It helps them to establish healthy and mindful eating habits as they grow, rather than turning into mindless 24/7 grazers.

It's your moral responsibility to provide healthy, balanced meals for your child. The more he learns to eat well right now, the more he's likely to do so into adulthood.

As he approaches one, you want to make sure you are feeding your baby the proper balance of solids and liquids so he gets all the nutrients he needs. For some babies, that means two bottles (or breastfeeds) along with solids, for others three. It depends on when he wakes and how hungry he is.

WEANING OFF THE BREAST

At around one year, if not before, most women stop breastfeeding but if you want to do it beyond then, that's your choice. Emotionally, Mum needs to be ready to give up. If you're not, question whether your reactions are healthy and in the interests of the baby. I have seen toddlers walking over to the breast and have known that they're using the breast as a pacifier. There's a point where instead of nurture and bonding between the baby and the mother, there's a complacency – she has become just a milking machine. Then it's time to cut it off as there is nothing to be gained here that's a healthy progression.

If your baby is eating solids regularly and getting fluids from a cup or bottle and you want to stop breastfeeding, cut the feeds down to one in the morning and one in the evening, if that isn't already the case. Then skip the morning feed and don't offer the breast again till the evening. If you taper off, you'll find your milk supply dwindling as well.

If your baby stops abruptly, you may go through a painful period where your breasts are engorged. Wear a nursing bra until the pain subsides, and use ice packs or bags of frozen peas covered in a tea towel on your breasts to reduce pain. In a few days, the milk production will stop and the pain will disappear.

WEANING OFF FORMULA

Bottle-fed babies should also be weaned at around a year to reduce the possibility of iron deficiency. This process should begin with weaning from powdered formula to cow's milk. Over several weeks, lower the formula and up the cow's milk in his bottles. Here's a table to show you how:

WEANING OFF FORMULA	
Week 1:	6 oz (170 ml) formula, 2 oz (55 ml) cow's milk
Week 2:	5 oz (140 ml) formula, 3 oz (85 ml) cow's milk
Week 3:	4 oz (110 ml) formula, 4 oz (110 ml) cow's milk
Week 4:	3 oz (85 ml) formula, 5 oz (140 ml) cow's milk
Week 5:	2 oz (55 ml) formula, 6 oz (170 ml) cow's milk
Week 6:	1 oz (25 ml) formula, 7 oz (200 ml) cow's milk
Week 7:	all cow's milk

Once he's drinking all cow's milk, he's probably ready to graduate to a sippy cup. You're about to be bottle-free!

WEANING ON TO A SIPPY CUP

Around the one-year mark, or perhaps a little before, it's a good idea to wean off the bottle or breast to a sippy cup, making sure, of course, that your child still gets his daily intake of milk, which by now should be 16 oz (450 ml). Gradually replace his bottles of milk or milk feeds with the equivilant amount in a sippy cup. You can also add milk to the food itself.

Weaning is another exciting developmental stage for you and your baby. It's an indication that he's entering the wonderful world of toddlerhood. More big changes are ahead.

SLEEP

One of the biggest mistakes people make is to say when their baby learns how to climb out of his cot, 'Oh, it's time to put him in a big bed.' No it's not. It's time for you teach your baby how to stay in his cot. He's not ready for a big bed. Place him in a sleep bag in the cot without toys except for one cuddly. When he climbs out, put him back and say, 'Stay in your cot and sleep.' If he cries, use the Controlled-Crying Technique (see page 177).

By now you've got a solid sleep schedule of a morning and afternoon nap and a full night's sleep. Here are two possible routines you might follow –

CORNERSTONE ROUTINE 9–12 MONTHS

By this time, the baby should be used to the habit of regular meals and enough naps in the day to give him a good 10 to 12 hours of sleep in the night.

Time all feeds from when the baby begins to feed.

7am	Breastfeed 20–40 minutes or bottle-feed 8–9 oz (225–255 ml)	You still need to make sure that they get their full intake of milk, which is 16 oz (450 ml) a day at this point. As you approach the one-year mark, try and wean the baby off the bottle and onto a sippy cup, but make sure the volume of milk doesn't drop.
9.30am	Breakfast	Breakfast should be baby cereal with milk, or pureed fruit. You might also offer the appropriate formula milk in a sippy cup. Afterwards, he should have a nap of about an hour.
10.30am	Snack	Offer a piece of fruit or perhaps a yoghurt at this time.
1pm	Lunch with dessert	Your baby may show signs of wanting to feed himself. Encourage him: it may be messy but it's also good fun and important for development. Give a good balance of protein, carbohydrate and full-fat foods, and include finger foods. You should also give the baby water or very well-diluted fruit juice. Water is best, though!
3.30pm	Snack	Some babies do better on three milk feeds a day rather than two. If so, offer them milk at this time rather than a snack. Afterwards, all babies should have a good nap.

| 5.30pm | Tea with dessert | If the baby has eaten a good portion of protein at lunch, you may feel it is not necessary to include it at supper also. But make sure this meal is still nutritious, balanced, and brimming with vitamins, and include a dessert to replenish all the energy spent getting into mischief. Try to make sure mealtimes are regular and take place in the baby's high chair to help them get into good habits. |
| 7pm | Breastfeed 20–40 minutes or bottle-feed 8–9 oz (225–255 ml) | Ready your baby for bed after his feed: after a bath, cleaning teeth and story he should be all set to sleep right through. |

fill in the times yourself. Be aware that your baby will test boundaries around sleep time between 8 and 13 months. You may have to use the Controlled-Crying Technique again.

GETTING OFF THE DUMMY

As I mentioned earlier, for a variety of reasons I think babies should be weaned off their dummies by around a year old for daytime, 18 months for sleeping. If you've only used it as a sleep aid, that won't be too difficult.

By now he's settled into a good sleep pattern and has the ability to go to sleep on his own. Begin by putting him down for naps without the dummy. After a few days of that, don't give it in the evening either. Here's a great chance to introduce a bedtime story and a cuddly stuffed animal or other soft bedtime cuddly toy to the routine. Tuck him in with his cuddly and say, 'Night night.' Gone with the dummy.

If your baby has been using the dummy during the daytime as well, you want to get rid of it, at least during the day, as soon as he's started to make words, so that he can communicate verbally. Begin by giving it only at night and then wean him off that as well.

Obviously it's a different story when we're talking about babies who suck their fingers or thumbs. Normally the child who has a dummy is the child that doesn't suck his thumb. If your baby intensely sucks fingers or thumb, then obviously it all wrinkles up like a prune. At this point it's best just to ignore such behaviour. If you see chafing, make sure to apply lotion to prevent cracking.

SETTING BOUNDARIES

Your little one is far too young to understand right from wrong or complicated reasons why he shouldn't crawl out of the window, so you should never try to reason with a baby, and you should never spank a child, but you can begin to teach him boundaries through your tone of voice. This is not permission to yell! Rather, to indicate disapproval, state firmly in a low tone, 'No, we don't smear food on the cat,' and then remove him from the temptation. And don't forget to keep praising everything he does right! The more you praise for what you do want, the more you'll get the behaviour you want to see.

PARENTCRAFT

HOLDING AND CARRYING

Even at this age, you should still be spending lots of time holding your precious one close to you. Most of those 'special moments' are right there in the middle of silence, just the two of you as he puts his little fingers on your face or presses gently on your eyelids, exploring your features.

Around nine months, there might be a little siding where your baby might express a preference about who he wants to be held by. Normally it is with the person he spends the most time with. If this is you, Mum, make a point of not being available sometimes so that your partner gets a chance to continue to develop a bond too. For the sake of some parents who don't want to admit it openly, I have something to say: you may like the fact that your baby is crying for you and not your partner because it flatters your ego, and he may say he doesn't mind. But please put the shoe on the other foot and understand what it must feel like. As a parent, you can't help but take it personally. So do what you can to make sure your baby stretches out his arms for both of you.

> 'It's your moral responsibility to provide healthy, balanced meals for your child. The more he learns to eat well right now, the more he's likely to do so into adulthood.'

BATHING

At this age, I like to have fun while washing babies' hair. I stick a play mirror on the tiles of the bathtub so they can see their hair sticking up like a Mohican or slicked back. It's all about creating fun together – but only if your baby has lots of hair, of course! Some still have minimal locks.

If he walks early, he'll probably want to start standing up in the bath, so be very careful. It doesn't take much for a baby to slip and bang his head. Hang on at all times! Seated is best.

DRESSING

This may be a time when dressing or undressing can be quite difficult because your baby refuses to let you change him. Again, we're looking at distraction. When your baby can stand or is pulling himself up on furniture, lay him down to get his nappy on, then let him stand up to get dressed while you're sitting down – he can lean on your shoulders while you pull up his trousers. Then have him sit down while you put on his shirt. Pull him up again to lean on you while you pop the poppers. He'll actually find this fun because he'll be quite pleased with himself for being able to stand and get dressed, and all the ups and downs will keep him stimulated.

From this time on, I love putting little soft-soled booties on babies' feet – you can get them in cotton, suede, corduroy or leather. Put them over Babygros or an outfit.

FIRST SHOES FOR THE EARLY WALKER

Once your baby becomes a confident walker, which is usually six to eight weeks after he has started consistently walking around, it's time for proper shoes. You'll know when he's ready because his toes will be flat on the floor. You can encourage this by taking his socks off so that he can balance better. This is quite an exciting time because it's another milestone. A lot of people save their baby's first shoes as a memento, and some even get them cast in iron or framed.

Go to a shop that provides fittings for both length and width. Shoes should have about 0.5 inch (1.3 cm) of room beyond the toe and be wide enough for all the toes to lie flat, and the heel should not ride up. Because your baby is so young and won't be able to undo his own shoes, it doesn't really matter whether they're buckle or Velcro, although Velcro is easier for you. First shoes should be very light, with a lightweight rubber sole so your child is able to lift up his foot. If the shoes are too heavy, your baby will clomp around like Frankenstein. Avoid plastic shoes because they don't allow feet to breathe.

The official Start-rite shoes are not cheap! However, it's essential that you get good-quality shoes from his first walking pair throughout toddlerhood and beyond. You've got to remember that even though your baby's walking, the bones in his feet are still soft, so it's incredibly important for that first pair of shoes to be the right fit. So many parents opt for fashion instead of looking out for their children's feet. Lots of brands cater for new walkers. Choose a proper shoe over fashion.

VISITS TO THE DOCTOR

Of course you've been to the doctor with your baby for his regular check-ups and if

TAKING A TEMPERATURE

From nine months onwards, you can take your baby's temperature by placing a digital thermometer under his arm. This can be a godsend as he may now be quite strong in protesting against the anal one. Be sure to read your thermometer's instructions, because how long you hold it there and what reading is normal varies.

he has caught an infection, but now your child's a lot bigger, moving around more, and most likely experiencing, 'This is a new place. I don't remember here and I don't like it,' so going to the doctor's for the one-year check-up is another scenario you need to plan for.

Make sure you take his changing bag with a few things in it that will keep him occupied. If an injection is needed, it's always better to have your child sitting on your lap facing you so that you've got eye contact and can talk to him with your arm round his shoulders and upper torso and his legs straight across your lap. This allows the doctor or nurse to give the injection in the thigh, which is the meatiest area.

BABYPROOFING

The goal at this time when it comes to babyproofing is to make sure your baby is safe but free to explore. Check locks on cabinets and doors. Tack down loose rugs so that your soon-to-be walker won't slip or trip. In the kitchen, make sure there are no chairs or step-stools near the stove that he can climb up on.

Make sure your garden is safe. To avoid a drowning hazard, empty the paddling pool after every use (your baby has probably had a wee in there anyway) and store upside down. If you have a swimming pool, it must have an electric cover or a self-closing and self-locking fence or other safety device to prevent accidental drowning.

Make sure the sandbox has a cover to keep cats out. Get rid of poisonous plants or teach your baby to avoid them. Make sure playground equipment is anchored properly and meets safety standards. Never mow the lawn, use a weedspray, or barbecue when your baby's outside.

STIMULATION AND EXPLORATIONS

By this point your baby is moving around and exploring more. He may be holding on to the knobs of lower cupboards and coffee-table edges. He may even have started to use a few words. Whether he's speaking or not, his capacity for communication is a lot stronger – he makes it as clear as possible by pointing. In this period, you're concentrating even more on crawling, climbing and pulling-himself-up games.

Because separation and stranger anxiety are strong now, you want to engage him in activities that will engross him as a way of distracting him from anxiety. At about one year, he may begin to form an attachment to a soft animal, blankie or other cuddly toy. These are great anxiety-reducers.

Remember to keep on giving solo playtime. By one year, you're looking at him spending about ten minutes engaged in an activity if he really enjoys it.

PLAY IDEAS
Talking for two

This can be a frustrating age for little ones because their minds sort of know what they want to say but verbally they're not there. Your job is to turn everything into a question and then answer it yourself to help him link actions with words. Double up on everything you say: 'Do you want your hat? Would you like your hat? Do you want me to give it to you? Here it is.' You may end up feeling like a parrot talking to yourself, but it's all part of being a parent: proposing questions and answering them to teach him how to respond to what you're saying.

Even though you'll be encouraging your child to talk more and offering him choices – 'Do you want the red one or the blue one?' – he's not going to actually turn round and say, 'I'll take the red one.' He may just take one from the two you offer, but the more you talk, the more he's going to understand. By the age of about 13 or 14 months, babies grasp exactly what you're saying, even though they can't communicate back fully.

When he speaks his first words, they may not be accurate – 'ba-ba' for bottle, for instance. Be sure you respond as if it were correct, but use the correct word in response: 'Here's your bottle, darling.' In this way, he'll learn the correct word more easily.

If you speak more than one language at home, great! He'll learn both. But keep them separated, Mum with one, Dad with the other. I would suggest English and no more than one other language as you will compromise his basic English trying to teach three or four.

Pincer play

This is a time to really help your baby with his pincer grip – using the thumb and forefinger together. Wooden puzzles with little knobs are great for this, so are stacking cups, blocks or plastic rings on a stick. If you don't have a ring, you can take a paper-towel tube and have your baby put bangles on it – supervised, of course.

Climb, tunnel and hide

This is a great time to find an activity class where you can help him develop his social skills and support movement and coordination by having him crawl in tunnels, over big foam blocks and under parachutes. Stairs are what your child will really want to climb, so make sure he's always supervised. Teach him to come down by showing him how to back up and reverse, then take it one leg at a time with you behind. Walking in and out of little tents and Wendy houses built under tables and chairs makes for a lot of fun too.

Push-toys

I like those little walkers that babies can push, because you get two in one. They're able to push and steady themselves as they're beginning to walk, and at the same time they usually come with an activity board.

Musical instruments

Music is incredibly important and something that I use consistently, beginning at the newborn stage, to soothe babies. At this age it's great to give your baby some maracas, a tambourine, triangle or little drum. It will bring him hours of fun, and will allow him not only to make music, but to grasp rhythm as he moves his body to the beat. His little personality will shine out. There are lots of different types – leather, metal, plastic: you decide.

You don't actually need to buy instruments. I like to get lots of assorted dried pulses, like lentils and chickpeas, and place them in different-sized plastic containers with sturdy lids. Your baby can grasp and shake them to hear the different noises. Again, be sure you supervise when this is happening as it is dangerous for a baby to eat the pulses.

Water, water everywhere

Babies of this age typically love water, whether in the bath or in a bowl. They love getting their hands wet and being able to put things in water and splash around. Yes, it may be messy, but find a time in the day for water play. Lay down towels if need be, and do it with them – for both safety and fun.

Big motion games

This is the time for big motion games, like flying aeroplane, bouncing on your knee, being swung under the armpits (never by the hands – you can dislocate a shoulder or break an arm that way).

Americans have Radio Flyers, those little red travelling wagons that you can pull little ones around in. You could use a big cardboard box or a plastic laundry basket to push or tie a rope on to and pull indoors or out. I spent a lot of time doing this with babies of this age, and they went through their toddler years enjoying it just as much. It's great to use sound as well: 'Vroom, vroom, vroom, you're a car; whoo, whoo, you're a train and chug, chug, you're a boat.'

Don't be afraid to take your baby to the playground at this stage, put him in the baby swing and gently push him back and forth. This is also the time when you can lift him lightly up into the air and catch him, or place him on a roll tube or large ball and move him from side to side or to and fro.

All these are games that not only allow you to connect physically, but reinforce the trust between you.

Where's the . . .

Now's the time to start playing visual memory games. You can show a simple board-book picture and ask, 'Where's the duck? There's the duck.' By around 12 months, he'll start to associate the name with the picture, as well as what sound it makes. The ground is being set for when he's a few months older and surprises you by saying, 'Quack, quack.'

PART 3

Exceptional
Circumstances

Contents

Chapter 8

Multiple Births

Wow! You're the parents of more than one bundle of joy! And you're in good company – there are more than 9,000 multiple births a year in the UK, mostly as a result of fertility treatment. And now, because of ultrasound, the fact that there's more than one will not be sprung on you in the delivery suite. You have time to prepare, which is good news. Needless to say, you'll have more than a handful! Get plenty of rest before the birth so you'll have as much energy as possible afterwards. I know you'll find multiples are a real blessing, and this book will help you feel at ease throughout the first year.

I've looked after twins as a nanny. In fact, the job I had just before I started *Supernanny* was looking after twin girls. Multiples still hold a fascination for people. They'll stop you in the street and ask, 'Who was born first? Who's elder? Oh, they are adorable!'

Because of IVF and other fertility treatments, many parents of multiples are older. These parents tell me that it takes very little to wear them out and they think it's because of their age. I always say, 'How do you know?' If you're on the older side, it's true that you may not have the stamina you had when you were in your twenties, but you have something else – maturity, stability and patience, the things that people learn along the way. Those qualities will help you make this year a joyful experience.

No matter your age, let me reassure you about one thing: I can definitely say from experience that things get easier after nine months on every level. Once your babies are older and you can turn them round in their bouncy seats, they'll amuse each other. There is something really special about the relationship between multiples, whether identical or not – a wonderful connection with each other that is a joy, not only for them but for you.

For the most part, the first year for parents of multiples is the same as for one, except that you're multiplying it all – multiplying the joy, multiplying the juggling, multiplying the need for a routine and the need for help. In this chapter, I will highlight those things you need to consider in addition to what I've written in the rest of the book. If your multiples were born early or are smaller than average, please also read Chapter 9 on premature babies.

EQUIPMENT
Your decisions about equipping the nursery may be different as you must consider

money, space and practicality for more than one baby. Obviously you're going to need more equipment, but that doesn't mean you need double or triple of everything. Don't buy more than necessary. There's only a certain period of time during which you're going to need this early equipment and then it's going to be useless, for a while at least. You're certainly not going to be thinking about needing it again for some time after just giving birth to two or three kids, that's for sure!

For instance, a car seat each is, of course, essential, but you only need one nappy-disposal container. You can only change one child at a time, so one changing mat is fine unless you plan to use more for simultaneous baby massage. Bottle-fed babies typically go through eight bottles or so a day, so depending on how many you have, you're going to need more bottles, but you don't need double or triple the number, if you sterilise more often.

I would definitely recommend each baby having her own Moses basket and cot, or at least her own Moses basket. Many parents think that because multiples have grown together in the womb, they would be better off sleeping together. I disagree, because there's always one baby who's more dominant. Just when you've got them off to sleep, the most dominant will make a noise and wake up the other(s). If they sleep separately, each has the chance to get the sleep they need. More importantly, some research has indicated that sleeping together may increase the risk of Sudden Infant Death Syndrome (SIDS). Since being a multiple is itself a risk factor for SIDS, I strongly urge you to put your babies to sleep by themselves on their backs, all swaddled nicely.

For triplets, I like the prams that have one seat behind the other rather than side by side. They're long, but they're not too wide to fit through the doorways of shops. I call them stretch limos. The side-by-side ones, however, are great if you want to go jogging. Nobody's going to get in your way, are they? You'll feel like you're driving one of those military tanks – nobody will mess with you when you're on the kerb! Shop doors have been getting wider and becoming automatic, making it easier to get in. I think they've realised that if you can't get in, you won't be buying anything. (In other words, no mummies shopping on impulse!) If you opt for a side-by-side pram, be sure it has one long footrest rather than two, because babies' feet can get caught in the gap.

Individual slings, seats, swings and bouncy chairs will come in incredibly handy and enable you to get things done more easily. They will also allow your babies to do things together, which is part of the fun of your unique situation – although don't put one baby in the front and one in the back of a single seat, please.

When it comes to toys and clothes, I believe it's nice for them to have some things the same and some different, and when there's only one of something, it will help them learn to share. In the long run, group activities are nice if they all have balls and rattles, but, for instance, they can all babble in a baby ring together.

Look ahead and stock up. Have a couple of spare cases of nappies and formula so you're never stuck in the middle of the night saying, 'Achh! I've run out!' Don't buy like a hurricane's coming, but definitely have a little bit extra just in case. Each time you go shopping, buy one extra thing, especially of the two-for-the-price-of-one specials. It's a way of creating an emergency supply without creating a big dent in your pocket.

PARENTS' JOURNEY

From the beginning, you'll start to recognise how very different your babies are as little human beings. Each has her own temperament and personality. Be sure you identify those differences as strengths and don't compare one with the other in a negative way – you'll find they complement one another. You need to be able to give each what they need emotionally and developmentally. With the help of your partner, friends and family, be sure to spend some time alone with each, even just a little while. It will allow you to really identify their little characters, which can sometimes fall into the shadows when you've been so busy just trying to keep track of it all 24/7.

Be honest with yourselves about the toll on the two of you, because dealing with two or more is very demanding. Keep talking about how you can support one another, so that each partner doesn't always feel overwhelmed. Remember it's the two of you raising the babies together. If you have other children, it can feel like you're running your own crèche. I know a family that has two sets of twins plus an older child. With minimum help, they've done fine and so will you.

At the very beginning especially, you want to have at least one or two more pairs of hands. A mother's helper is really good, or a nanny, doula or relative – any kind of additional supportive help. The more assistance you can get, the easier it will feel (see Useful Addresses on page 263).

Becoming overloaded with everyday needs can leave you forgetting about yourselves. Be kind to yourselves, please. When you feel brave enough, take that step and book a night out, even if it's only a quick meal. Of course, most parents of multis under nine months old would rather chill on the sofa with a take-away. Do that too. I've babysat while parents were in the living room taking a few hours off.

It also helps to meet with other parents in your circumstances. There are wonderful groups of parents of multiples you can join as well as special websites that can offer emotional and practical support (see Useful Addresses on page 263).

However many children you're juggling, be aware that everything will take more time: time to get everyone out through the door, time to feed everyone, and so on. You're running a production line – multiple bottles, baby food, laundry. The more kids you have, the more organised you need to be. As the babies get older, it will all take less time.

Work out your priorities – what you can and can't let go of. Do you need to wash every day, or can it be every other day? Is it essential that the telly gets wiped over every day, or can it go for a week? If you can afford it, get a cleaner in. I know many women who feel so proud to say, 'I do my own cleaning.' Swallow your pride and don't polish the martyr crown!

There's a lot of fun to be had with multiples. You'll find yourself totally amazed that these babies are yours. You'll have days when everybody is cooing over your babies – how beautiful they are and how they should be modelling. These moments compensate for the times when you're up at three o'clock in the morning thinking, 'Oh my God, there are two (or three or four) of them! Well, they always said be careful what you wish for.'

I'm not going to harp on about how tired you'll be because you know this already. It is to be expected – you're human, not a robot – but I want to emphasise again the importance of an upbeat mentality. You can create a lifestyle that works for you and your new family. Expect the smooth as well as the rough, the positives as well as the negatives. Focus on what you want, not on what you don't. Have a positive mindset so you can enjoy parenting these amazing children of yours; so that you can enjoy this new stage of your lives and be proud, confident parents.

I've very much enjoyed looking after twins. Very much. I believe it will bring out the best in you. You have to learn to adapt very, very quickly. You think on the hoof and learn to multitask. Pretty soon, you're a seasoned parent of multiples, able not only to adjust to any challenge, but to enjoy yourself in the process!

Oh, and I forgot to mention – eyes do grow in the back of your head . . . Or maybe it just seems that way.

DEVELOPMENTAL OVERVIEW

Even if they are visually identical, you will find that each baby develops at their own pace. You may see that one turns over, sits up or starts to talk sooner than the other, or that one is able to pick up her spoon and feed herself before the other one. This is where, as a parent, you want to be sure to treat each as an individual, which means that you see the potential in the one who's ahead and build on that, while encouraging the other. You may find that the one who talks earlier ends up doing the talking for both of them, so make sure you encourage each at whatever rate they're progressing.

You need to be aware of their differences and respond to each baby without getting frustrated or fearful about the differences. This is exactly the same as what you would do if you had one baby who was developing at a different pace from a friend's baby. Check with your doctor if you're truly concerned.

You may find your babies have different tastes in food as well, or that one eats more than the other. Emotionally, they may respond to things differently – they will each have her own temperament and personality. One child might cry at fireworks and the other not. I can't tell you how many parents of newborn multiples say to me, 'They may have been in the same sac, but they are individuals.' And of course that's true – separate souls, separate hearts. Again, it's your job as parents to enjoy the differences as well as the similarities and to support each child as they become themselves. Different strokes for these little folks, most definitely.

As they get closer to a year, you'll notice that they will begin to pay a lot of attention to one another. The way they nicky-picky over each other is wonderful, and the way they fuss over things together is wonderful as well. Putting them together in a big baby gym is a great way to observe how they interact – touching one another's faces, gurgling and smiling together. Or not.

From the start, multis are used to having another person around 24/7 and their social abilities develop very quickly as they are able to communicate with another little person about everything all the time. Sometimes I've watched how they make each other laugh with a facial expression or squeal. It's healthy to let them just be together sometimes.

The funny thing is that when they reach about a year, you go into neutral and they find their balance with you. They find it, not you. They work out their balance with one another, and with you.

SETTING FIRM GROUND

In the beginning, parents have great intentions to treat each baby separately when it comes to eating, sleeping and playing. That all goes out of the window after about three weeks as you realise the bags under your eyes are looking like double cheeks. That's why I suggest – for your health and sanity – that you feed them at the same time, as then they'll sleep roughly at the same time.

Just as you would with a single baby, establish a sleep and feeding routine so you can manage your time more efficiently. Again, that means flexibility within routine. If your twins are on their afternoon naptime and one wakes up ten minutes before the other, you don't make that one stay in the cot for ten minutes and try to get her back off to sleep; you get her up earlier. It may mean that you run ten minutes earlier with feeding that one too. The slight variations in their schedules will allow you to have one-on-one time with each.

FEEDING

One way to make your life easier while still providing the immunity of breast milk is to use a pump and give it in bottles, supplemented by formula if need be. Or breastfeed at home and give them a bottle when you're out and about because it's easier and you want to make your life as easy as possible. Another benefit of bottles is that you'll know exactly how much each is getting. Of course it's your decision. Some mums of triplets who've chosen to breastfeed have told me that it helps them bond emotionally with each of them.

If you have twins and decide to breastfeed, the best position, as shown in the illustration, is with both babies on V-pillows with their legs facing your back. Make sure you're very comfortable because you're going to be there for at least half an hour. Switch which breast each baby suckles so that you don't get flatter on one side if one feeds more than the other. Plus it'll give them a different view! You can wind them at the same time by simply turning them over across your lap together.

When they start on solid foods, parents always ask me, 'Which one do I feed first?' Just take turns: today I fed you first for breakfast; now I feed you first for lunch. No favourites. One of the marvellous advantages of having multiples is that they learn early about taking turns and sharing. You can line them up in their high chairs and go down the line. Of course, if you don't have a high chair for each, then they really have to take turns. They may not like it, but hey, ho . . .

PARENTCRAFT

One of the facts of having more than one baby is that if you are by yourself and changing one, you can't be changing the other, so one might cry a bit longer. Again, take turns. Make sure that the more dominant one doesn't always come first just because she's making the most noise. Give the one who's waiting a toy to hold on to.

Try not to beat yourself up about not being able to respond instantly. Your children are going to learn a little bit more patience earlier because of their circumstances and that's very healthy. They won't do everything at the same pace. For instance, one may be slower at eating so the other will have to wait.

As much as possible, make it easy on yourself by bathing each on alternate days to lessen the chore. Or do them together and have every other day off. Trim their nails at different times depending on the rate of growth.

Divide up the tasks between you and your partner – laundry duty, cooking and so on. When both of you are there, each of you can take primary charge of one baby, alternating so that you both get time with each. Or one of you takes them both so that the other adult gets a real rest. You'll soon see what works best. With triplets or more, holding and carrying them simultaneously is virtually impossible. With twins, it's a bit easier – two hips, two kids; but that will create back problems, so try not to do it.

A quick tip is always to place yourself in the middle so they learn to share you: two legs to sit on, two arms, thank God. Around nine months, they will get a little possessive about wanting you to themselves. I would suggest you approach this with, 'There's room for all of us,' unless it's that special one-on-one time, which is so crucial at this period because almost all of their time with you is shared. During this period especially, be sure to find ways of giving them individual attention without the other around.

As much as possible, do all the things you would do with one, like baby massage. With two, put yourself in the middle with one on each side of you on a blanket on the floor. You can stroke each back and tummy at the same time. With more than two, rotate them.

EXPLORATION AND STIMULATIONS

Because multiples develop at different paces, your job as a parent is to provide the stimulation each needs. That may mean moving the more developed one on to more advanced toys or games because otherwise she'll get bored if she's waiting for her twin to catch up. Keep her moving forward while you're encouraging the other one to get to where she already is.

When they become mobile, you've really got to be careful – you've got more than one to watch like a hawk. This is where a playpen can come in handy. Put them in together for about ten minutes while you grab a bite of lunch or go to the toilet, but don't overdo it. Using a playpen as a babysitter is neglect.

Enrol them in activities with other babies and see if a relative can come with you, or alert the staff that you will need an extra pair of hands at the class. With swimming, you absolutely need one adult for each baby.

If one becomes ill, the other must follow in tow. Your primary job is to get your little one better. (Only to find out that the other has it the following week, right?)

You're really earning that badge

There's a saying that if you learn to drive in London you can drive anywhere because the city is so busy and the streets so narrow. When you learn to raise twins, triplets or quads, at the end of the first year you've passed the parent test blindfold! The saying that two's company, three's a crowd is not true in the baby world. It's two's a pair, three's a party. Olé!

Chapter 9
Premature Babies and Other Special Needs

Congratulations! Just like every other parent reading this book, you've just given birth to a wonderful new baby. Yours just came a bit early, or with a health issue, which means she needs special treatment. I want to encourage you to get all the practical and emotional support you need to feel more at ease during the first year and beyond. There are lots of resources, information and support available (see Useful Addresses on page 263), but I also want to offer my thoughts so that you can be a confident parent and enjoy this first year as much as possible, because, like every other parent, you deserve to!

In the beginning, it might not be easy for the two of you to digest all the information you may be bombarded with. You may be experiencing lots of mixed emotions. Whatever your circumstances and however you may be feeling, I believe every baby is born with a healthy spirit. It will be your job to recognise that beauty beyond the mental or physical realm so that your child will be loved and nurtured without a shadow of a doubt. In the process, you will, as parents, learn to put everything else into perspective.

PREMATURE BABIES

DEVELOPMENTAL OVERVIEW

Premature babies are born pre-term, meaning before their due dates. The longer a baby stays in the womb, the more it can develop. Some babies, even though they may be born three to four weeks early, don't seem to be behind developmentally.

Usually, however, if your baby was born prematurely, she's smaller and more fragile than other newborns. The good news is that due to medical advances, even babies born at only 28 weeks have a 95 per cent or better chance of survival. She's just going to need special medical care around the clock, especially if she was less than 3 lb (1.3 kg) at birth.

Premmies' weight is measured in grammes and the reason they must be incubated is that they have little or no body fat and so must be kept warm. Often premmies have breathing issues because of immature lung development. They're more likely to have jaundice, abnormal blood sugar and hernias. These things clear up as they get older, with medical attention.

If they're extremely premature, they may be born covered in down, which will fall out. They may look more wrinkled and fragile as they have not yet developed muscle on their bones. Depending on how premature they are, they may also have translucent skin, a bald head, sealed-shut eyes and may not have nipples. Their blood vessels may be visible under their skin. Never fear – as they grow, they will look more and more like the baby you were imagining.

Because she's not gone full term development-wise, you need to take care of her once she comes home in such a way as to enable her to play catch-up.

Generally speaking, she'll be behind for the amount of time she was premature. If she was born two months premature, for instance, at four months, she'll probably be at the two-month stage of development. Each baby catches up at her own rate, and usually becomes age-appropriate by two or so, although some continue to have a bit of a lag after that. They often grow in spurts.

HEALTH ISSUES

Because your baby's immune system is less developed, be sure you check before bringing small children to visit her in hospital. Keeping your baby clear of infection is extremely important for her health, and catching a cold is twice as harmful as it is with a baby who's fully developed.

At home, you should restrict visitors, at least at the beginning, and keep your baby away from crowds. You need to keep a close watch on any fevers, and you will probably have more regular visits from the home health visitor to make sure your baby's doing okay. Premmies are at greater risk of ear and eye infections, and may have hearing problems. If your baby doesn't jump at loud noises, see your doctor.

PARENTS' JOURNEY

Don't be afraid to ask all the questions you need. The staff in the neonatal intensive-care unit are trained to help you as well as your baby. Having a premature baby can be very scary for parents, particularly when she's hooked up to all those tubes and monitors in hospital. You may feel anxious or depressed that you have to go home and leave her there, especially if you have other little ones at home already. See if you can trade off with other family members so that someone is always there and you get time to recover. Hold her, especially skin to skin, as much as possible. It's good for you and for her.

I've taken care of premature babies and realise that, as parents, you have to deal with the feeling that your baby is fragile. It's easy to be concerned, even after she's been approved to leave hospital and come home. Be aware that, realistically, your baby's not going to be let out of hospital until the doctors feel that she's safe to be released in good health. If you don't already know it, learning infant CPR can give you greater peace of mind. I strongly recommend it to every parent, not just those with premmies.

Many women feel that it's their fault that their baby was born prematurely. They worry that they caused it somehow: did they eat something? Do something? Not do something? No one knows for sure why it happens. Try not to blame yourself. It was out of your control.

FEEDING

Because premmies have less fully developed immune systems, you can give your baby a great health boost by breastfeeding if at all possible. However, some babies born prematurely have trouble feeding because they've been born before the sucking reflex develops (that happens somewhere between 32 and 34 weeks) and aren't yet able to latch on. If this is the case, she will be fed through a nose tube in hospital. Be sure to have skin-to-skin contact and have her nuzzle your breast in any case so that she'll be ready to breastfeed when the reflex kicks in. Your doctor may suggest vitamins and minerals, especially iron, to supplement breast milk or formula.

Premature babies need to be fed more often than full-term ones – as much as ten feeds a day to prevent dehydration. If she has six to eight wet nappies a day, you know she's getting enough. She may spit up more, which may interfere with her weight gain. Talk to your doctor or health visitor if you're concerned.

OTHER ISSUES
Baby seats

One thing to be aware of with premmies is that research has shown that they can develop breathing problems if left in a seat for long periods of time. Talk to your doctor about this. Keep trips in the car short and make sure someone is sitting with your baby when you're driving to check on her breathing. It's also recommended that you recline the seat as much as possible while still following the car-seat manufacturer's guidelines, and make sure her head and body aren't slumped over. Never leave her alone in the car, and don't put her in a baby seat while in the house. Use the Moses basket or a sling.

Clothing

As I mentioned earlier, one of the other key issues with premmies is that they need to be kept very, very warm because they have little or no body fat. At home, you need to dress her in two layers more than you ordinarily would until she reaches 7.5 lb (3.4 kg). There are special clothes and nappies for premature babies because they're so tiny.

Sleep

Understand that your baby is going to sleep even more than a full-term baby as that's what she would have been doing in the womb – sleep, sleep, sleep. Sleep is the best thing your baby can do in the beginning to catch up, but be prepared for your baby to sleep for shorter periods of time between waking.

Crying

Premmies may cry less than other babies because they don't have the physical strength. Instead, they may shut down more easily, so beware of overstimulation – or the opposite.

Routines

Apply all the routines I suggest in the Setting Firm Ground sections later than if your child were full term – later with scheduled feeds, later with solid food, later with sleep schedules. How much later depends on her size when born and how quickly she's catching up. To gauge it, go by her developmental age, not her physical one. This is particularly important when adding solids, because premmies may choke more easily and have immature digestive systems.

OTHER SPECIAL NEEDS BABIES

Because of prenatal tests, it's likely that if you have a special needs baby, you knew in advance. However, whether you were prepared or surprised, the most important thing to remember is that this is your baby. Just because she's been born different from the 'norm' doesn't mean that she should receive any less of your attention or love. If anything, she should receive more because of her medical circumstances.

That's why I would make sure that, above all, the two of you receive counselling, both to accept the medical condition that your child has been born with and to get support for the condition itself. I would encourage you to find out about everything you can do to make life as normal as possible.

Ask your doctor as many questions as you want as many times as you need. Make a note of the answers if need be. Ask if your child is eligible for an early support programme and whether there is a child development centre in your area that can help. Your doctor and health visitor will know what services are available. Ask if her condition will get better or worse over time. You may qualify for a Disability Living Allowance. Ask about that too. Find out as much as you can.

Even if you knew from day one what you were getting into, you'll be dealing with varying emotions. It's one thing to know that your child has cystic fibrosis or multiple sclerosis, Down's syndrome, spina bifida or a congenital heart problem; it's another thing to deal with it in reality. The reality will hit, for instance, that your baby is not as responsive as she would be if she didn't have this condition.

There are really two kinds of extra work – the emotional work of acceptance and the physical work of caring for a baby with special needs. You have to accept 'This is what my baby has' and then work on being the best parent that you possibly can and giving your baby the upbringing that she deserves. So much of it has to do with your mindset – your determination not to let your emotions tear you apart, but rather to find out all you can to give your child the very best. I've seen, for example, babies that have been born with Down's syndrome end up doing extremely well because of the incredible continuous care they received from their families.

That doesn't take away the very real demands of a child who's got special needs, because those are real; but take it on as a challenge to be faced, while making sure you're getting care and support as well, because you are going to be with other parents who have children that don't have medical conditions and you're not going to be able to help but compare. You'll look and think, 'My child's not doing that.' But you'll know why. And you'll know what you can do to give your child the healthiest and happiest life possible.

Give yourself time to adjust to this new reality. If you find yourself becoming depressed, be sure to get help. Listen to those around you if they suggest you get support. Your doctor can help you find a support group or a counsellor; so can the Useful Addresses on page 263. Be aware that you and your partner may be at different parts of the journey of acceptance at any one time. Listen to how each other feels and get support as a couple if you need it. Find ways to have time together apart from the baby.

DEALING WITH SIBLINGS

Having a baby with special needs can be difficult to explain to a young child but it's not really necessary because in her limited understanding it's not any different from having a 'normal' sibling.

If the sibling is older, she's better able to understand. As the older sibling grows, she's able to recognise that her younger brother or sister needs more help, and, just like you, will be able to develop more patience, understanding and empathy as a result of being part of your special family. They can end up developing good qualities that might not otherwise have come until adulthood. That's what makes this journey unique, but please be patient with your other children too as they're learning at their own pace.

DEALING WITH OTHER PEOPLE

One of the challenges parents of special needs babies face is dealing with the comments and questions from others. Only you can find your way with this. Especially with strangers, don't feel obliged to go into a whole long explanation unless you feel like it. If people make remarks that offend you, walk away.

When it comes to family members, understand that they have to go through their own process of acceptance and are asking questions out of concern. If you know what you need from them in terms of support, ask. If they offend you, teach them how you want to be spoken to about the situation. This is an area in which being in a support group can really help. Above all, have a positive mindset. Parents of special needs children surprise themselves with the understanding, compassion and empathy they develop. It takes someone special to raise a special needs child, and I believe that one day you'll look in the mirror and know that person is you!

Chapter 10
The Adopted Baby

Just like every other parent, you're finally holding the baby you've been waiting for. Just like every other parent, you're saying, 'I am ready to take on the responsibility of being a loving parent and raising my child to be a loving human being.'

I think I know a bit of what you're feeling because I have a somewhat similar experience as a nanny. Some of the babies I've looked after are now teenagers. I've never looked after any baby with less moral responsibility, delight, nurturing or loving than I would my own, and that's something that's really hard to explain, because people always say, 'When you've got your own, it's different.' Maybe that's true for those who feel that babies have to biologically come from them, but aren't babies a blessing full stop? I know you can love and care for your baby regardless of where she's biologically come from. More than anything, because of the whole elaborate process of adoption I think that if ever there was a conscious decision to have a child, it was made by parents who adopt.

I know that, like other parents, you're going to worry about her health and well-being and, at times, about whether you're up to the job. Like other parents, you've got to work out feeding schedules and routines. Like other parents, you're going to feel emotional on occasions because it isn't just pregnancy hormones that make you feel overwhelmed. Otherwise, how would fathers feel the same?

I know that you want the best for your baby. Almost every word in this book applies to you. You're going to need as much patience, confidence and love as any other parent. I've chosen to include a chapter on adopted babies because I want to raise some issues for you to think about based on the unique way your child came into your family. In particular, you need to take into account the age of the child and his history before making decisions about schedules, sleeping arrangements and stimulation.

GETTING YOUR BABY

There's one key difference between you and other parents. When you meet your baby, you're not as worn out as a biological mother, so you don't have that lack of energy and emotional tiredness that you have if you have given birth vaginally or gone through a C-section.

Instead, you're probably excited. You're ready for a little party. If your baby is newborn, you can easily overwhelm her with your energy, so be aware that she needs her rest. And remember that soon you're going to be hit by the fatigue too. Whether you're breastfeeding or bottle-feeding, you're still going to have to deal with those nights when your baby is waking up, wanting to be fed on demand.

If your baby is older when she's adopted, she may be feeling confused or upset. Who is this new person who's holding her? Where is the person who has been caring for her? She may cry a lot in those first days and/or refuse one or the other of you. You may be afraid she won't love you. Don't worry – as you care for her, her connection to you will grow.

If possible, get as much information about her history before you adopted her, as well as any genetic or other medical information that may be relevant to her health as she grows. If it's not an open adoption, see if you can arrange a way to trace the birth-parents if you ever need to for a health problem. If this isn't an option because your child was abandoned, remember that the need for such information is rare, so try not to worry too much about it. You just want to know as much as possible so you can do the best possible job as a parent.

BONDING

Many adoptive parents get very anxious if they don't immediately connect to their baby. Actually, it has nothing to do with giving birth, as many biological parents who don't automatically bond will tell you. Just like biological parents, you may be swept away by a sea of emotions, creating waves of positive and negative feelings – fear, inadequacy, exhilaration, love, the realisation that your life will never be the same. Understand that these are the feelings of parenthood, not caused by the route you used to become parents.

As I have said in earlier chapters, some people bond instantly; others need time for the relationship to develop. Don't scare yourself that it's all to do with the fact that she's adopted. Whether you birthed them or not, babies come with their own little ways of being and might not be what you imagined. It's no different from biological parents who say, 'Oh, I wanted a boy, and now I've got a girl.' You grow in love over time with the one you have. If you continue to worry about this as the weeks and months go by, or feel that your child is not bonding with you, please get help from your doctor, who can refer you to the right support.

'The important thing here is just to respect that your little baby is unique and very, very special. In your own time, together you will bond.'

It's very easy as a parent to find excuses for why you're not bonding with your child if he's adopted. It's human instinct to come up with reasons why, especially when you've waited so many months to receive the baby that you have wanted so badly. The important thing here is just to respect that your little baby is unique and very, very special. In your own time, together you will bond. I say 'in time' because that's exactly what it's going to take – time. No relationship bond is a deep one unless the time is put in to really connect.

POST-NATAL DEPRESSION

Yes, adoptive mums can become depressed. It may not have hormonal components, but the difference between your ideas about how you would feel and the reality can trigger a downward spiral. You may experience feelings of inadequacy and of being overwhelmed, anxiety and maybe negative thoughts about yourself and your baby. It may physically manifest in sweats and heart palpitations or feeling very lethargic. If you experience any of these or other unsettling feelings or thoughts, I would strongly advise that you talk to somebody close to you, and if that doesn't help, that you reach out and talk to your local GP, because, without help, you can spiral downward quite seriously.

DEALING WITH INFERTILITY

Many adoptive parents have had a tremendous number of tries at getting pregnant before choosing adoption, so dealing with their infertility is something that a lot of adoptive parents must come to terms with. Some people think they've dealt with their grief only to feel it very strongly when they get their baby. Women, in particular, may feel sorrow that they haven't given birth to this child, or about not being there for the first months if their baby is older.

Why is it that you feel incomplete? Is it that you haven't experienced giving birth or gone through the stages of carrying a child? Is it that you feel bad that you've not been able to biologically have your child yourself? Hopefully you've reached an acceptance of that before the baby arrives, but if the feelings get stirred up again, do get support. And remember, this is what you've been waiting so long for – your baby is here, even if it didn't happen in the way you imagined.

Millions of families have been happily created by adoption. Feelings of infertility grief are a normal process for some parents. Understand that you're going through a phase, and get help so that you can move on to the more positive feelings that come from giving a child a place within your home and in your heart. Get moving with it so you can enjoy parenthood to the full.

BREASTFEEDING

These days there is a trend towards adoptive mothers taking hormones in order to breastfeed their babies or towards buying breast milk from others to give their newborns antibodies. It was well known when I was born that my mother shared her abundant supply of breast milk with women in the ward who had none. So I say, who am I to knock anyone who gets breast milk for their baby from someone else? Each to their own really. The main thing here is to do what's best for you, and not to judge another mother's decisions.

When it comes to injecting hormones, that's a decision that should be made only after advice from a doctor. What are the possible side effects of taking such hormones? I would also most definitely advise any woman considering such a step to talk to someone on the emotional level as well, to explore why she wants to make that choice. Millions of babies have done just fine on formula. Are you doing this for the baby or for you?

OPEN ADOPTION

A lot of people have open adoptions in which the adoptive parents agree to stay in contact with the birth-mother and/or birth-father. If you're in this situation, be prepared for emotional times during the first year for both parties. It takes a level of maturity to do this properly. Everyone must focus on the baby's well-being, not on the emotional needs of the adults. If you find that one of the adults is not on an even keel, then by all means have an open discussion so that person can get extra support, which is incredibly healthy, not just for all the adults involved but for the baby, too.

It certainly is possible for open adoptions to work well. I know of a person who was a teenager when he had a baby and was unable to care for her and now has a wonderful relationship with his daughter and is very close to her adoptive parents. Be sure everyone in the situation has support to help them make wise decisions and help them through the feelings.

Here are my suggestions for making open adoption work for everyone, especially your baby:

- Make sure your expectations of each other are clear.
- Establish what the child will call each person – who gets to be called Mum and Dad? What will the others be called?
- If you don't have a written communication contract, it's a good idea to create a verbal one. It should spell out how often there will be communication and in what form – letters, calls, photos, visits?
- The agreement should also spell out who, if anyone, in the birth-parents' families will be in contact – grandmothers, grandfathers, and so on.

Be aware that you are entering into a relationship that will evolve over time. Many birth-parents end up using the phone as the main mode of communication. They want to hear about how the baby is doing, but are uncomfortable around the adoptive family because of unresolved feelings. Adoptive parents, on the other hand, may feel threatened by the birth-parents, feeling less 'real', and will look for ways to distance themselves. Some birth-parents disappear after a couple of years; some stay connected for ever. A lot of this you will have to decide as you go along, keeping the needs of the child left, right and centre. Be prepared to continue to make mutually agreed-upon decisions.

Some periods may be easy, others challenging. Like any relationship, you will learn what to expect from one another and discover more and more about what works best for you all.

SURROGATES

I feel strongly that people who use surrogate mothers and gay people who have women bear children for them (or have friends as sperm donors) should be clear about keeping an open relationship. Again, the well-being of the child should come first; my suggestions regarding open adoption apply here too.

ADOPTING A BABY OF A DIFFERENT NATIONALITY

In the first year, any issues of nationality are totally irrelevant to your baby, but you do have to be prepared. You have to understand that you're now a bi-racial family, and this has implications for you and your child in the future – wonderful and positive implications. Your baby's heritage will encourage you to research another culture just as you would if you married someone of a different nationality.

INSTITUTIONALISED BABIES

Many children, especially those adopted from places like Russia, Romania, China, Vietnam and Cambodia, have been institutionalised before being adopted and may be delayed physically, emotionally and intellectually as a result of neglect. These infants are generally not adopted as newborns, but at six, nine or twelve months. These babies may have been starved. If that's true, it's important to give small quantities of food at very frequent intervals so she doesn't develop bad habits like hoarding food.

It's also important for you to know if your baby's delayed so that you can get going on helping her to catch up. Even if you don't know her history, you can tell from significant physical, emotional or mental delays. Generally, neglected children are undersized and seriously behind in development.

If your baby is delayed, you need to step back a bit, as if you're dealing with a premature baby. For instance, if you receive a child when she's one year old, if her development is behind, you go back and parent as if she's much younger. Her calendar age is less important than her developmental age. Even more than with other babies, what's important is that you're seeing progress, not how she compares with others on a chart.

As the parent of an abandoned or neglected baby, your job is to make her feel incredibly safe and secure so that she can trust you, because, with trust, she'll start to connect emotionally with you and then start to explore the stimulations you place in front of her. This will give her the competence to reach those milestones.

'The most important thing, as it is with any baby, is creating those harmonious times when you and your child can enjoy yourselves.'

The most important thing, as it is with any baby, is creating those harmonious times when you and your child can enjoy yourselves. You're both laughing and enjoying the stimulating play, whether it's creating body awareness or eye–hand coordination or developing listening skills or visual tracking. The fact that you're doing it with her is what's significant.

As a parent, what matters the most is feeling a great determination to get your baby back on track. It's like you're coaching her on that mile-long run so she can end up at the finishing line. I encourage you to see it as a very exciting rather than a fearful thing: 'Okay, I'm going to marshal all my love and all my attention to give her a boost-up!' Focus and commit 100 per cent to bringing your child up to scratch. The hard work you put in now will pay dividends later.

ADAPTING MY ADVICE

During the first year, the baby's 'job' is to develop a sense of basic trust in the world. This trust develops through the bond, or attachment, she makes with her caregivers. As a result of interruptions in this bonding process, especially in cases of abuse and/or neglect, some adopted children develop attachment problems. Symptoms in infants are either that they are too good – they never make demands and rarely cry, and are content to entertain themselves for hours – or that they are inconsolable and reject comforting from parents, and don't make eye contact or imitate parents. If your baby is exhibiting such symptoms after the first month or so, be sure to see an attachment specialist or family therapist. You can find one through your adoption agency, or talk to your doctor.

To minimise the possibility of attachment problems, especially if your child was abandoned or neglected, I would recommend the following modifications to my advice in other chapters:

• Consider keeping your baby next to you in a cot or a co-sleeper (one of those things that attaches to the side of your bed) longer than other infants. She will get great comfort from your physical presence.
• Keep her on you in a sling more than you might otherwise.
• I would not use the Controlled-Crying Technique. Often these babies were abandoned at night and so sleeping is challenging. Under the circumstances, if she cries, pick her up and soothe her, no matter how many times. Eventually she'll feel safe.
• Your baby may experience night terrors – screaming, kicking and thrashing while asleep – as a result of trauma. Again, pick her up and soothe her as best you can. One thing that works is to wake her up, reassure her, and then put her down again.

Babies who have been abandoned and neglected need you to spend as much one-to-one time with them as possible. You have to really gain your baby's trust – in the hands she was in before, that trust was broken. That's what you're doing here. You're creating a safe haven for your child so that she feels she can totally depend on you and trust the stability of your care. Dancing with your baby, doing massage, rolling her across an inflatable ball, lifting her up high to touch something, doing the famous Superman flying through the air – all of these activities will allow your child to understand she can trust you to hold her. Of course all the peek-a-boo games should come a lot later because of the insecurity of being left alone.

Above all, the best thing you can give your infant is consistent caring that will show her she can count on your love and depend on you to meet her needs. And that's no different from what all parents should be doing!

TALKING ABOUT ADOPTION

The time has long passed when the advice was to hide the fact that your child was adopted. As an infant, of course she can't understand – it doesn't really kick in until at least age four – but many parents worry even when their child is an infant about when and how to discuss it. I believe you'll feel in your heart when it's the right time, and that won't be until your child is older. Live in the moment and enjoy this first year of having your baby. That's what you should be focusing on now.

You can set the stage for a positive experience by talking to your little one right from the start about the day you met her, and by creating a scrapbook which details your adoption journey, how you came together and what you, as parents, were feeling, just like birth-parents do.

This book will be a little treasure chest for when she is older. Rest assured it will become one of your child's favourite books! All children like to hear, as they get older, how their parents met and where they were from. These stories help them to answer important questions such as 'How do I fit in?' and 'Where is my place?'

SUPPORT GROUPS

One of the realities of adoption is that it doesn't matter to you, but it does to your child. This is not relevant in the first year, but is something you need to be aware of right at the start. For you, it may be an unbelievably positive experience, but one day your child will understand what adoption means and will have an ambivalence about it that you don't have.

This doesn't mean she won't love you as much, but she will begin to think things like, 'How come my birth-parents didn't want me? There must be something wrong with me.' And if it isn't an open adoption, 'Who am I biologically? And what are my birth-parents like?'

While these thoughts and feelings are way down the line for your child, one of the best things you can do right from the start is join a support group of parents and children in similar situations so you can find like-minded people to connect with. There are lots of organisations for families with babies from around the world. Try your adoption agency for starters. You want to be able to get the best knowledge, support, and suggestions that you can.

Above all, though, just as I say throughout this book – please relish this wonderful time with your new baby! Getting her off to a good start will go a long way towards creating a solid parent–child relationship that will be your joy – and hers.

And finally:
The One-Year Milestone

There's no doubt that every parent says it: 'My God, that year went too quickly. Where did the time go?' While you were going through it, you were aware that time was passing, but suddenly your baby's first birthday's here and you've got a few friends round the birthday cake and all the babies are crying because the noise from singing 'Happy Birthday' is too much and you're sitting there crying, 'I can't believe it happened so quickly!' Your baby has changed from a newborn to a one-year-old who's talking in one-syllable words and piling that cake into his mouth. Then you recognise how much you've matured. Okay, so you don't look like you did in your wedding photos, but you've also gained something precious – a maturity and confidence you didn't have before. As much as you listen to other people's opinions and take advice from experts, you trust yourself a lot more. You're able to recognise that inner voice, your intuition, and pay attention to it. You feel proud that you can hold your head up high and join the ranks of experienced parents. You're grateful for all you've learned this year and for the beautiful child before you, still in one piece. You realise he's his own person and not just an extension of the two of you. Congratulations! You can take those L-plates off – you've passed your first year! Now, ready or not, it's toddler time. But you are ready, you know you are, and that's the difference. A year ago, you weren't sure.

PART 4
Useful
Resources

Contents

GROWTH CHARTS

These can be found in the little red book, supplied by your health visitor.

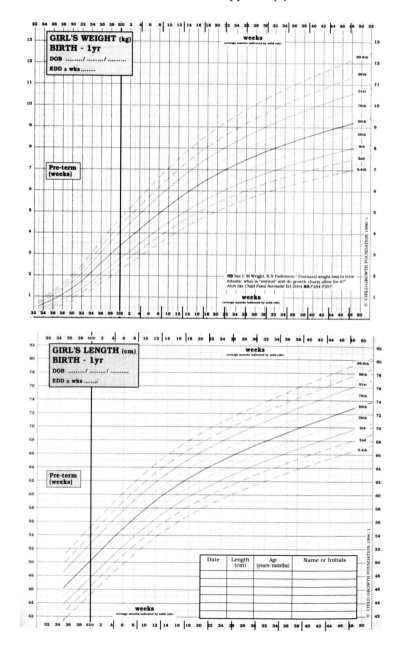

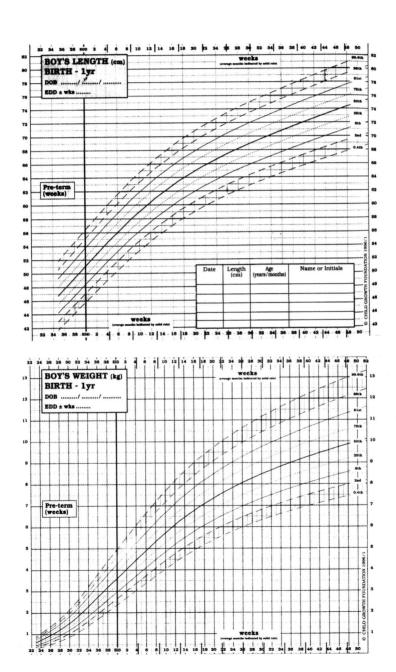

NHS-RECOMMENDED IMMUNISATION SCHEDULE

The recommended timetable for childhood vaccinations is:

At two months old:

- diphtheria, tetanus, pertussis (whooping cough), polio and Hib
- pneumococcal conjugate vaccine (PCV).

At three months old:

- diphtheria, tetanus, pertussis (whooping cough), polio and Hib
- meningitis C.

At four months old:

- diphtheria, tetanus, pertussis, polio and Hib
- meningitis C
- pneumococcal conjugate vaccine.

At 12 months old:

- Hib
- meningitis C.

At around 13 months old:

- measles, mumps and rubella (MMR)
- pneumococcal conjugate vaccine.

NON-ROUTINE IMMUNISATIONS:

At birth (to babies who are more likely to come into contact with TB than the general population):

- Tuberculosis (BCG)

At birth (to babies whose mothers are Hepatitis B positive):

- Hepatitis B

COMMON ILLNESSES AND AILMENTS

This is by no means a comprehensive list, but it will give you an idea of what to do if you encounter some of the more common illnesses or ailments. I recommend getting a good infant medical care book that gives more detail and treatment suggestions.

ILLNESS/AILMENT	SYMPTOMS	ACTION
Acne	Small red bumps on the skin that appear shortly after birth, due to the overload of hormones	Will clear up.
Asthma	Coughing, rapid breathing, rapid movement of the muscles below the ribs, flaring of nostrils, wheezing, bluish tint to lips or nails	Call the doctor. Call an ambulance if there is difficulty breathing.
Bronchiolitis: infection of the smaller passages of the lungs	Runny nose, mild cough, fever; then after a couple of days the cough becomes worse and breathing laboured	Call the doctor. Call an ambulance if there is difficulty breathing.
Cold	Runny nose, mild cough, sometimes fever	Use a humidifier. Call the doctor if fever rises above 100.4°F (38°C).
Conjunctivitis: also known as pink eye or sticky eye	Swelling, redness, discharge in the eye(s)	If newborn, call the doctor immediately as it is very contagious and can be linked to pneumonia.

Useful resources

ILLNESS/AILMENT	SYMPTOMS	ACTION
Cradle cap	Scaly patches on the scalp	Will clear up. Apply olive oil and comb through.
Croup: inflammation of the voice box and windpipe	Whistling or barking sound when breathing or coughing; may turn blue when coughing	Call the ambulance if there is difficulty breathing.
Diarrhoea	Loose stools more than six times a day, discoloured	Call the doctor.
Ear infection: infection of the inner tubes of the ear	Irritability, especially at night; may pull or bat at ear; fever	Call the doctor.
Eczema	Reddish skin that oozes and becomes scaly; caused by allergy or contact with something irritating	See the doctor.
Fever	High temperature, sweating	Call the doctor if temperature rises above 100.4°F (38°C) or if there are other concerns such as lethargy, poor feeding.
Flu	Dry cough, sudden fever, chills and shakes	Call the doctor if temperature rises above 100.4°F (38°C).

ILLNESS/AILMENT	SYMPTOMS	ACTION
Gastro-oesophageal reflux	Vomits after eating / pain during or after feeds	Wind often and keep upright for 30 minutes after feeding; see a doctor if it's excessive or persistent.
Heat rash	Small bumps that appear when exposed to sun or heat	Keep cool and dry; apply calamine lotion.
Heatstroke	Dangerous! Suddenly raised temperature due to getting too hot, – e.g. on the beach, in the car, being overdressed in hot, humid weather CAN CAUSE DEATH	Cool body down ASAP (undress, sponge or wet with cool water) and RING AN AMBULANCE OR GO TO A&E.
Hives	Itchy red, raised bumps that look like welts, either all over the body or in one area; may be caused by allergic reaction to food, pollen, drugs, insect stings or infection	Call the doctor.
Impetigo	Bacterial infection: small red spots appear, usually on face, neck or hands. Highly contagious	Call the doctor.
Ingrown nail	Redness around the nail	See the doctor.
Jaundice	Yellowing of the skin and whites of eyes	Will clear up if mild; if it persists, see a doctor: may need a sunlamp for a few days. In the first

ILLNESS/AILMENT	SYMPTOMS	ACTION
		few days, discuss with your midwife or health visitor. Definitely consult your doctor if it persists for 2–3 weeks. If it occurs any time after the first four weeks, see your doctor as it is more likely to have a non-physiological cause.
Jitters	Shaking of the whole body/part of the body	Call the doctor.
Pneumonia: a viral or bacterial lung infection	Cough, rapid breathing, rapid movement of the muscles below the ribs, flaring of nostrils, wheezing, bluish tint to lips or nails or tongue	Call the doctor.
Thrush	White patches in the mouth, redness of throat, baby off her milk	Call the doctor.
Vomiting		If excessive, projectile, accompanied by fever or diarrhoea, or goes on for more than 12 hours, call the doctor immediately. Dehydration may occur, which can be fatal.

MENINGITIS

Is your baby getting worse fast? Babies can get ill very quickly so remember to check them often. Not every baby gets all these symptoms, and they can appear in any order.

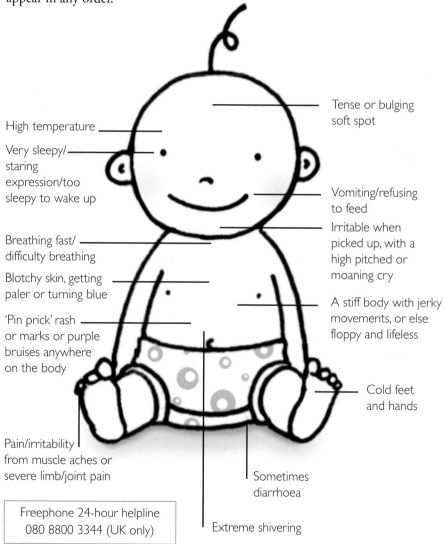

Tense or bulging soft spot

High temperature

Very sleepy/ staring expression/too sleepy to wake up

Vomiting/refusing to feed

Irritable when picked up, with a high pitched or moaning cry

Breathing fast/ difficulty breathing

Blotchy skin, getting paler or turning blue

A stiff body with jerky movements, or else floppy and lifeless

'Pin prick' rash or marks or purple bruises anywhere on the body

Cold feet and hands

Pain/irritability from muscle aches or severe limb/joint pain

Sometimes diarrhoea

Freephone 24-hour helpline
080 8800 3344 (UK only)

Extreme shivering

EMERGENCY FIRST AID FOR CHILDREN UNDER ONE

I strongly recommend that every parent take an emergency first aid and CPR (cardiopulmonary resuscitation) class, available through St John's Ambulance or a private course. I'm including the basics here as a reminder only, not as a substitute for proper training. Reading about CPR is very different from performing it.

> **RULE NUMBER ONE IN ANY EMERGENCY:**
> Keep calm, call for emergency help and stay with the baby.

Burns

- Run cool water, not cold, over the burn until the pain subsides – up to 20 minutes. Do not use ice.
- If it's first degree (redness, slight swelling, no blistering, major swelling or charring), apply a gauze dressing.
- If it's second or third degree (blistering, a lot of swelling, or charring), is caused by electricity or chemicals, or is on the face or eyes, leave it uncovered and go to hospital. Or consider covering with clingfilm.
- Do not immerse the baby in cold water.
- Do not remove clothing.

Choking

- If the baby is coughing, crying or breathing, do nothing. Do not offer fluids – they may block the air passage more.
- If the baby is not breathing, call an ambulance immediately and:
  - Place your baby face down on your knees and push rapidly and firmly five times with the heel of your hand between his shoulder blades to expel the object.
  - If that doesn't work, put him on his back on the floor and, using two fingers, press his chest at the breastbone five times in quick succession, about 0.5 inch (1.21 cm) deep, being careful not to injure his ribcage. (See illustration of infant CPR on page 261.)

Cuts or scrapes

- Hold under cool running water.
- Remove any dirt with clean tweezers under running water.
- Apply pressure with a piece of gauze until the bleeding subsides. If blood seeps through the gauze, add another piece on top.
- Dress with antiseptic cream and cover with a plaster.
- If the cut is deep or bleeding, doesn't stop quickly or you can't get the dirt out, get emergency help.

Head injury

- If it's a tumble that produces a knot (egghead bruise), an ice pack should do the trick.
- If you suspect a serious head injury or an injury to the spine, do not move the baby but call an ambulance immediately. Stabilise the baby while waiting for help by placing your hands on either side of her to keep her head still, keeping the head and neck in a neutral position.
- If the baby is throwing up, roll her whole body over to prevent choking and protect her neck and spine.
- If she's unconscious, check to see if she's breathing. If she's not, administer CPR while waiting for an ambulance. (See illustration of infant CPR on page 261.)
- If there's bleeding, apply pressure with a nappy or other cloth until bleeding stops, then apply an ice pack to reduce swelling. Heavy bleeding from the scalp does not necessarily mean a serious wound because there are lots of blood vessels close to the surface. However, if you can't stop the bleeding or if it's severe, call an ambulance.
- If you suspect a skull fracture, do not apply pressure.
- If the skin is broken and there is dirt in the wound, do not clean. Cover with gauze and seek immediate medical attention as head wounds can cause brain infections.
- If her eyes are crossed, or one pupil is dilated more than the other, or she's been unconscious even briefly, get emergency help immediately.
- For 24 hours after any head injury, your baby should be monitored for unconsciousness, vomiting or trouble breathing. To be on the safe

side, consult your doctor. You may be advised to wake her every few hours to make sure she's not unconscious.

Heat stroke

• Take the baby to a cool place and remove all clothes. Bring down her temperature immediately with a cool sponge bath or immersion in cool bathwater and fanning while you call for emergency help.

Insect stings

• Apply a cool compress until the pain subsides.
• Remove the stinger, if there is one, by scraping it with a credit card. Do not use tweezers as this may force it further in.
• Watch for infection – streaks of red or yellow – or signs of allergic reaction:
  ◦ unconsciousness
  ◦ difficulty breathing
  ◦ hives or itching over the entire body
  ◦ swelling of the eyes, lips or penis

If you see any of these signs, call an ambulance or go straight to A&E.

Poisoning

• Take away the substance and remove any from the baby's mouth. Save some for analysis.
• If she's drooling, sleepy, having trouble breathing or is convulsing, call an ambulance immediately.
• Otherwise, call your doctor or hospital, describe the symptoms and follow their instructions.

INFANT CPR

If your baby is unconscious, call for emergency help and check for responsiveness by tapping gently on her chest, shoulders or feet. If you get no response, do ABC:

Airway: Quickly check to see if she's breathing – look, listen and feel for signs of breathing. If not, tilt her head back so her nose is pointing up. Be careful not to put her head too far back as this can block an infant's air passage. (See illustration 1.)

Breathing: Cover the baby's mouth and nose with your mouth, creating a seal. Gently and quickly give a puff of air, then remove your mouth and watch and listen for an exhalation. (See illustration 2.) If there's none, repeat with one breath, covering her nose and mouth. If she's still unresponsive, check:

Circulation: Place two of your fingers for three to five seconds at the brachial artery, which is located inside her upper arm, between the elbow and the shoulder. If you do not feel a pulse within that time, then her heart is not beating and you will need to do chest compressions.

Compression: Place three fingers in the centre of her chest with the top finger on an imaginary line between her nipples. Raise the top finger up and gently but firmly compress with the bottom two fingers. You can easily damage the ribcage if you press too hard. The compression should be approximately 0.5 inch (1.2 cm) deep. (See illustration 3.) Count aloud as you perform *five* compressions and follow up with two breaths. Repeat this cycle 30 times before checking for breathing and pulse.

If there is no pulse, continue administering five compressions to two breaths until an ambulance arrives. If at any point the infant regains a pulse but still does not breathe on her own, give her one rescue breath every three seconds.

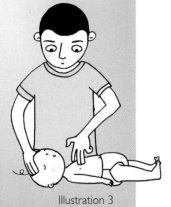

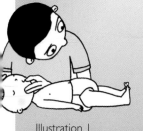

Illustration 1

Illustration 2

Illustration 3

FIRST-AID KIT

The following items are the things I consider to be essentials for the first year and beyond:

- antiseptic cream for scrapes and cuts
- arnica for bruises
- cotton wool
- fever-reducers like Calpol. Be sure to consult the doctor before giving it, especially to babies under three months. Never give aspirin to children as it is linked to a serious liver disorder called Reye's syndrome.
- first-aid manual
- gauze dressings to clean cuts and stop bleeding, and adhesive tape to hold it in place
- ice pack – small and large. The new flexible ones that don't require freezing are great. Just twist and they're cold.
- Infacol
- oral syringe or droppers for giving medicine
- plasters in various sizes
- rehydrating fluids like Diarolyte in case of infant diarrhoea
- rubbing alcohol for disinfecting tweezers, and tweezers for removing splinters, glass, etc.
- small scissors
- thermometer – digital rectal.

USEFUL ADDRESSES

Adoption
Adoption UK
www.adoptionuk.org.uk
Online and face-to-face support for adoptive parents before, during and after adoption.

Allergies
The Healthy House
www.healthy-house.co.uk
0845 450 5950
Lots of information and products for an allergy-free and non-toxic household.

Breastfeeding
Association of Breastfeeding Mothers
www.abm.me.uk
0844412 2949 (hotline)

Breastfeeding Network
www.breastfeedingnetwork.org.uk
0870 900 8787

La Lèche League
www.laleche.org.uk
0845 456 1855

Childcare
Sure Start
www.surestart.gov.uk
0700 000 2288
Offers free information about childcare services, including finding the right nanny or childminder.

Working Families
www.working families.org.uk
0207 253 7243
0800 013 0313 (legal advice line)
Offers valuable information and advice on flexible working hours, childcare and employment rights for working parents. Has local groups throughout the UK.

Dads
Baby Centre
www.babycentre.co.uk/baby/dads
This general website has a special section for new dads to share their thoughts and feelings with one another and get support and information.

Brand-new Dad
www.brandnewdad.com
An online community for expectant and new fathers.

HomeDad UK
www.homedad.org.uk
Devoted to fathers who are stay-at-home dads.

Doulas
DONA International
www.dona.org
Offers information about what birth and post-natal doulas do and how to find one anywhere in the world.

Gear

Kiddicare
www.kiddicare.com
Offers a wide variety of the top brands of
baby accessories, nursery equipment,
carriers, toys, etc., including equipment for
multiples.

Grandparents

Good Granny
www.goodgranny.com
A website by and for grandparents,
'especially the young-at-heart grannies of
today'.

Grandparents Association
www.grandparents-association.org.uk
The first UK charity devoted to
grandparents.

Grandparents Magazine
www.grandparentsmagazine.net
Online articles and resources.

Seniors Network
www.seniorsnetwork.co.uk/grandparents
News, views and features on issues related
to grandparenting.

Health Concerns

NHS Direct
www.nhsdirect.nhs.uk
0845 46 47
Offers a 24-hour nurse helpline, or go to
the website for a health encyclopaedia.

Multiple Births

Multiple Births Foundation
www.multiplebirths.org.uk
0208 383 3519
Information on the care, development
and special concerns of multiples.
Clearing house for other associations,
like Home-Start.

Twins Club
www.twinsclub.co.uk
By parents of multiples, for parents of
multiples – find clothes and good baby
equipment for multiples as well as lots
of advice and shared experiences.

Twins and Multiple Births Association
www.tamba.org.uk
0800 138 0509 (helpline)
Information and support for parents
of multiples.

Nanny Searches

Here are three top nanny-search firms:
www.nanny-search.co.uk
www.nannyjob.co.uk
www.nanny-agency.com/UK-nannies

Nappies

There are two sources for finding
a nappy service:
The National Association
of Nappy Services
www.changeanappy.co.uk
0121 693 4949

UK Nappy Helpline
01983 401 959

Post-natal Depression and Social Isolation

Association for Post-natal Illness
www.apni.org
0207 386 0868
Telephone support for mothers with post-
natal depression and an information
website.

Home-Start
www.home-start.org.uk
This charity is run by a network of parents
helping others struggling to cope for
whatever reason – post-natal depression,
loneliness, multiple births, illness, etc.
Will link you to a local group.

Meet-a-Mum Association
www.mama.co.uk
0845 120 3746 (helpline, Mon–Fri
7 pm–10 pm)
Will put you in touch with other mothers
who have dealt with post-natal depression
for support and resources.

Mind (National Association
for Mental Health)
www.mind.org.uk
0845 766 0163 (infoline)
Confidential helpline for those in mental
distress. The website can direct you to a
Mind association near you.

Premmies

Fertility Zone
www.fertilityzone.co.uk
This website has parenting boards for
parents of premmies to share feelings and
get support.

Mongabay
http://health.mongabay.com/conditions/
    Premature_Babies.html
Offers a wide selection of articles on
premature babies as well as places to get
help.

Safety

Child Accident Prevention Trust
www.capt.org.uk
0207 608 3828
All kinds of information and resources for
keeping your child safe.

St John's Ambulance
www.sja.org.uk
27 St John's Lane
London EC1M 4BU
08700 104950

Special Needs

Come Unity
www.comeunity.com/disability
Clearing house for contact information for a
wide variety of special needs support groups
and information. The place to start to find
the group you need.

Contact a Family
www.cafamily.org.uk
UK-wide charity that provides information,
advice and support for families with special
needs children.

Support and Advice

www.JoFrost.com or
   www.b4ugo-ga-ga.co.uk
B4UGo-Ga-Ga
My website, where you can ask me
questions, share your learning with other
parents worldwide and get support.

Baby Centre
www.babycenter.com or
www.babycentre.co.uk
Track your baby's development online and
much more.

LovetoKnow Baby
www.baby.lovetoknow.com
This general website has a baby section where
you can share what you're learning about
your baby with other mothers and fathers.
Lots of information for adoptive parents
here too.

A Healthy Me
www.ahealthyme.com
All kinds of information on infancy and
parenting.

National Childbirth Trust
www.nct.org.uk
0870 444 8709
This charity offers courses and information
on all aspects of parenting and directs you
to post-natal groups and classes.

Parentline Plus
www.parentlineplus.org.uk
0808 800 2222
Free confidential helpline for parents who
have worries – minor or major – or are
struggling. The website can direct you to
parent classes and other resources and offers
support on a range of topics plus a message
board for discussing with other parents.

Toys

National Association of Toy and Leisure Libraries
www.natll.org.uk
0207 255 4600
Information about local toy-lending
libraries. Download their Good Toy Guide.

Baby Log

This is a place for you to record all the little things your baby does that you'll want to remember and will be helpful to look back on – like when they sleep, feed, poo. I have given you a template below that you might find helpful – copy it and you will find it very useful as a quick reference guide.

DATE

Time	Activity	Duration	Comments

DATE

Time	Activity	Duration	Comments

DATE

Time	Activity	Duration	Comments

Index

Index

PICTURE CREDITS:
Kevin Frazier: 25, 215; Daniel Pangbourne: 2, 3 8, 15, 45, 65, 135, 157, 181, 205, 223;
Philip Silcock: 1; Author's own: 6; Illustrations by Maria Smedstad/EyeCandy.